Pocket
MELBOURNE

TOP SIGHTS • LOCAL LIFE • MADE EASY

Trent Holden & Kate Morgan

In This Book

QuickStart Guide

Your keys to understanding the city – we help you decide what to do and how to do it

Need to Know
Tips for a smooth trip

Neighbourhoods
What's where

Explore Melbourne

The best things to see and do, neighbourhood by neighbourhood

Top Sights
Make the most of your visit

Local Life
The insider's city

The Best of Melbourne

The city's highlights in handy lists to help you plan

Best Walks
See the city on foot

Melbourne's Best...
The best experiences

Survival Guide

Tips and tricks for a seamless, hassle-free city experience

Getting Around
Travel like a local

Essential Information
Including where to stay

Our selection of Melbourne's best places to eat, drink and experience:

◎ **Sights**

✖ **Eating**

🍷 **Drinking**

✪ **Entertainment**

🔒 **Shopping**

These symbols give you the vital information for each listing:

📞	Telephone Numbers	👪	Family-Friendly
⊙	Opening Hours	🐾	Pet-Friendly
P	Parking	🚌	Bus
⊖	Nonsmoking	⛴	Ferry
@	Internet Access	M	Metro
📶	Wi-Fi Access	S	Subway
🌱	Vegetarian Selection	⊖	London Tube
🍴	English-Language Menu	🚋	Tram
		🚆	Train

Find each listing quickly on maps for each neighbourhood:

Bar Hemingway

16 🍷 Map p233, B2

Legend has it that Hem:
self, wielding a machine
ate this timber-pan
ered bar during
showpiece is a
en by Papa a
town. Dress
s.com; Hôtel Rit
: ⊙ 6.30pm-2a

6 ◎ *Plac*

Lonely Planet's Melbourne

Lonely Planet Pocket Guides are designed to get you straight to the heart of the city.

Inside you'll find all the must-see sights, plus tips to make your visit to each one really memorable. We've split the city into easy-to-navigate neighbourhoods and provided clear maps so you'll find your way around with ease. Our expert authors have searched out the best of the city: walks, food, nightlife and shopping, to name a few. Because you want to explore, our 'Local Life' pages will take you to some of the most exciting areas to experience the real Melbourne.

And of course you'll find all the practical tips you need for a smooth trip: itineraries for short visits; how to get around, and how much to tip the guy who serves you a drink at the end of a long day's exploration.

It's your guarantee of a really great experience.

Our Promise

You can trust our travel information because Lonely Planet authors visit the places we write about, each and every edition. We never accept freebies for positive coverage, so you can rely on us to tell it like it is.

QuickStart Guide 7

Explore Melbourne 21

Worth a Trip:

The Best of Melbourne 135

Survival Guide 157

QuickStart Guide

Welcome to Melbourne

Stylish, arty and cosmopolitan Melbourne is proud of its place as Australia's cultural capital. Stately gold-rush-era architecture and a multicultural make-up reflect the city's recent history, while edgy street art and sticky-carpeted band venues point to its present-day personality. It's also a top sporting city, playing host to Grand Slam tennis, Formula One and – its main obsession – Aussie Rules footy.

Centre Place (p31)
DAVID HILL / GETTY IMAGES ©

Melbourne
Top Sights

Federation Square (p24)

Geographically and socially, Melbourne's striking Fed Sq is the city's epicentre. It's a place to hang out, have a drink, people-watch and enjoy world-class galleries such as the Ian Potter Centre: NGV Australia and ACMI.

St Kilda Foreshore (p124)

Come to St Kilda for its sea breezes, seedy history, fascinating mix of people and lively nightlife. On hot summer days it's *the* place to hit the beach.

Birrarung Marr (p26)

A slice of tranquillity in the heart of the city, Birrarung Marr is a tribute to the Indigenous Wurundjeri people. It's great for a stroll along the Yarra accompanied by fantastic city views.

Melbourne Museum (p110)

Delve into the story of Melbourne, marvel at dinosaur fossils and learn about Indigenous Australia. At this museum you'll cover a broad sweep of Victoria's natural and cultural histories.

Melbourne Cricket Ground (p82)

In one of the world's sporting capitals, the MCG takes centre stage with 60,000-plus roaring footy or cricket fans attending match days. The museum is a must for sports fans.

Queen Victoria Market (p28)

Melbourne's historical central market is a great spot to shop for gourmet produce, and to take in the atmosphere of booming greengrocers spruiking their goods. Lively summer evening markets are a highlight.

NGV International (p48)

NGV is home to a collection of artwork that spans the globe and includes master painters Rembrandt, Monet and Picasso, plus exquisite Asian and African pieces. The gallery's blockbuster shows are a huge attraction.

Abbotsford Convent & Around (p106)

This former 19th-century nuns' convent is a hub of artistic activity, host to galleries, theatres, flea markets and cool cafes. Surrounding the convent is the Collingwood Children's Farm and attractive parkland.

Royal Botanic Gardens (p68)

Regarded as one of the finest botanic gardens in the world, this sprawling green space combines both native and non-native plant species. Picnic on its grassy slopes around the duck ponds.

Royal Exhibition Building (p112)

Melbourne's only Unesco World Heritage Site, this beautiful gem was built in 1880 for the International Exhibition. Book a tour to see inside, or just stand in awe of its grand facade.

Melbourne
Local Life

Insider tips to help you find the real city

After checking out Melbourne's top sights, here's how you can experience what makes the city tick – trendy city laneways, a thriving rock 'n' roll scene, hip inner-city suburbs, local designers, and an obsession with single-origin coffee and craft breweries.

Arcades & Laneways (p30)

▶ Street art
▶ Laneway bars

Once a no-go area of toppled rubbish bins, rats and X-rated theatres, Melbourne's laneways have undergone a dramatic transformation to become a celebrated part of the city. These days they're all about street art, Parisian-style cafes, hip restaurants and boutiques in 19th-century arcades.

Williamstown (p56)

▶ Maritime ambience
▶ Science museum

Jump on a ferry for a scenic trip along the Yarra to end up in the seafaring suburb of Williamstown. One of Melbourne's most historical neighbourhoods, here you'll encounter bluestone buildings, wide streets and a beautiful harbour bobbing with yachts.

East Brunswick (p90)

▶ Cafes
▶ Local hang-outs

Multicultural Brunswick and hip East Brunswick are just the places to explore genuine, cool hang-outs with a local vibe. Ceres is a don't-miss for anyone interested in anything sustainable, and you'll find plenty of craft beer, artisan coffee roasters and band venues worth checking out.

Fitzroy & Collingwood Pub Crawl (p94)

▶ Bars and pubs
▶ Late-night eats

The area may be hipster central, but don't let that deter you. This pub crawl takes you to true 'locals' that have been favourite watering holes for many years, complete with an unpretentious vibe and welcoming punters.

View of Melbourne from Williamstown (p56)

Fitzroy (p92)

Other great places to experience the city like a local:

Prahran Market (p74)

Cinema Nova (p121)

The Tan (p72)

Collingwood Arts Precinct (p98)

Thy Thy 1 (p86)

Rose Street Artists' Market (p105)

Windsor Castle Hotel (p76)

St Kilda Bowling Club (p128)

Pure Pop Records (p133)

Rosamond (p100)

Melbourne
Day Planner

Day One

Start in the city along stylish Flinders Lane with breakfast at **Cumulus Inc** (p38), before a spot of boutique shopping in the laneways and arcades. Take time to browse some of Melbourne's famous street art, most prominent down **Hosier Lane** (p34). Head across Flinders St to the city's heart, **Federation Square** (p24), for the free 11am tour of its complex. While here, visit the **Ian Potter Centre: NGV Australia** (p25), most popular for its Indigenous collection, or **ACMI** (p25), a more modern-day interpretation of Australian culture with displays on TV and film. Head across the road for tapas at **MoVida** (p138).

Jump on a tram to spend the afternoon in St Kilda. Enjoy sea breezes along its picturesque **foreshore** (p124) and grab a coffee at the pier kiosk. Check out **Luna Park** (p125) before a sundowner at **Republica** (p131) with views over the bay.

Head back into the city for Mexican street food at **Mamasita** (p38). Take a drink in laneway bar **Chuckle Park** (p41), before catching a show or having a night out on cocktails at **Bar Americano** (p41) or sweaty rock 'n' roll at **Cherry** (p31).

Day Two

Begin your day at the **Queen Victoria Market** (p28), browsing gourmet produce in its historic deli hall and taking in the lively atmosphere of the fishmongers. Grab something from the deli or create a picnic hamper for lunch in nearby **Flagstaff Gardens** (p37) or across town in the **Royal Botanic Gardens** (p68).

After a stroll through the botanical gardens, head across St Kilda Rd for quality art at **NGV International** (p48), featuring everything from Indian sculpture to Impressionist paintings. Then follow the banks of the Yarra through **Birrarung Marr** (p26), one of the city's best green spaces with Indigenous themes. From here cross the William Barak 'singing' Bridge en route to the **MCG** (p82), either for a weekend game or to visit its **National Sports Museum** (p83) and take a tour of the ground.

Head to Fitzroy for a sunset drink at the sensational rooftop bar at **Naked for Satan** (p100). Dine at **Charcoal Lane** (p99) for Indigenous-inspired cooking, then check out local watering holes on a **pub crawl** (p94), or more refined pursuits with cocktails at the **Everleigh** (p100). Finish in Collingwood with a local band at the **Tote** (p102).

Short on time?
We've arranged Melbourne's must-sees into these day-by-day itineraries to make sure you see the very best of the city in the time you have available.

Day Three

Begin the day by hitting the **Tan** (p72) for a jog or taking a brisk walk around sparkling **Albert Park Lake** (p62) – home to the Australian Formula One Grand Prix. Breakfast awaits at the **South Melbourne Market** (p62) in its artisan cafes and eateries, or opt for the boutique **Prahran Market** (p74), where you can sign up for a cooking class.

Head back into inner-north Carlton for the **Melbourne Museum** (p110) and World Heritage–listed **Royal Exhibition Building** (p112). Take a long lunch along Lygon St, Melbourne's Italian precinct, with pizza at **DOC Pizzeria** (p117) and espresso from **Tiamo** (p118). Spend the rest of the afternoon visiting animals at the **zoo** (p116).

As the sun goes down, get over to St Kilda to experience its notorious nightlife. Those who like to mix drinking with leisurely activities should head to **St Kilda Bowling Club** (p128) for cheap drinks and lawn bowls. For dinner try a seafood dish at **Claypots** (p129) or more upmarket cuisine at **Mirka's at Tolarno** (p130). Music fans should mark as essential a night at the **Espy** (p133), and beer lovers can try the **Local Taphouse** (p131).

Day Four

Grab a single-origin coffee and breakfast from **Proud Mary** (p101) and spend the morning shopping in Fitzroy and Collingwood along Gertrude, Smith and Brunswick Sts, stopping at **Third Drawer Down** (p103) and **Aesop** (p103). Head to **Abbotsford Convent** (p106) for its art galleries and cafes, and the **Collingwood Children's Farm** (p107), overlooking the river along attractive **Yarra Bend Park** (p107).

From here you can head to the suburbs to **Heide Museum of Modern Art** (p155) in Bulleen, which offers rotating exhibitions of Australian modernist painters such as Sidney Nolan and Arthur Boyd. Alternatively, from the city jump on a ferry to spend the afternoon in maritime suburb **Williamstown** (p56). Plenty of historic buildings lie along its main road overlooking a picturesque marina of yachts. While you're here, duck into **Sea Shepherd Australia** (p57) for a tour of its anti-whaling vessels.

Enjoy your night with a cheap and boozy Vietnamese dinner in Richmond at **Minh Minh** (p86), followed by a gig or a drink upstairs at the **Corner Hotel** (p87). Alternatively, head into Prahran/Windsor for a night clubbing at **Revolver Upstairs** (p76) on Chapel St.

Need to Know

For more information, see Survival Guide (p157)

Currency
Australian Dollars ($)

Language
English

Visas
Visas are required for international travellers; check www.immi.gov.au for information.

Money
ATMs widely available. Major credit cards accepted almost everywhere.

Mobile Phones
Local SIM cards are available and cheap. CDMA band phones don't work in Australia; other phones can be set to roaming before leaving.

Time
Melbourne is on GMT+10; during daylight savings (late October to late March), Melbourne is 11 hours ahead of GMT.

Plugs & Adaptors
Standard voltage is 240V/50Hz. Plugs are either two or three pins. International adaptors are widely available.

Tipping
Not obligatory but around 10% is standard in city restaurants and cafes and is appreciated in bars.

1 Before You Go

Your Daily Budget

Budget less than $80

► Dorm bed $20–$35, double from $60
► Cheap meal $7–$15; eat at food markets
► Art galleries and local gigs from free to $20

Midrange $80–$200

► Double room $80–$180
► Two-course dinner $40–$80
► Independent theatre from $50

Top End more than $200

► High-end boutique hotel room $200–$300
► Three-course dinner in a top restaurant $80–$200
► Theatre or opera from $80

Useful Websites

Lonely Planet (www.lonelyplanet.com/melbourne) Destination info, hotel bookings, traveller forum and more.

Broadsheet (www.broadsheet.com.au) Bar, cafe and restaurant reviews.

Visit Melbourne (www.visitmelbourne.com) Events, attractions, travel info.

Advance Planning

Three months before Book your hotel during main events.

One month before Book hostel rooms during summer, high-end restaurants and tickets for international bands.

A few days before Book tickets for local sports events and bands.

Arriving in Melbourne

Most international and domestic visitors arrive at Melbourne (Tullamarine) Airport. Avalon Airport is also used for domestic flights, so check your ticket carefully. Southern Cross Station is a main hub for long-distance trains and buses.

 From Melbourne Airport

Destination	Best Transport
Southern Cross Station	SkyBus runs express services every 10-30min
City centre	taxis $50; around 20min

 From Avalon Airport

Destination	Best Transport
Southern Cross Station	Sita Coaches meets every flight
City centre	taxis $80; around one hour

 From Southern Cross Station

Destination	Best Transport
City centre	train to Flinders St Station
St Kilda	tram 96 or 112; taxis $25, around 20-30min
Fitzroy/ Collingwood	tram 86 or 112; taxis $20, around 20min

 Getting Around

Melbourne is well connected by a network of metro trains, trams and buses operated by Public Transport Victoria (www.ptv.vic.gov. au). Ticketing is through the plastic myki card ($6), a 'touch on, touch off' system, which you put credit on before you travel. Purchase cards at major train stations and 7-Elevens. For more info, see p161.

 Tram

An extensive network of tramlines runs north–south and east–west along most major roads. Trams run every 10 minutes from Monday to Friday, every 15 minutes on Saturday and every 20 minutes on Sunday.

 Train

Flinders Street Station is the main metro train station connecting the city and suburbs. The City Loop runs under the city, linking the four corners of town.

 Bus

Melbourne Visitor Shuttle (www.thats-melbourne.com.au) visits all the city sights.

 Bicycle

Cycling maps are available from the Melbourne Visitor Centre (www.melbourne.vic. gov.au/touristinformation) at Federation Square and Bicycle Victoria (www.bv.com.au). For short trips, Melbourne Bike Share (www. melbournebikeshare.com.au) offers free 30-minute use of bicycles in the city area, though you need to buy a $5 safety helmet from a 7-Eleven store.

Taxi

Melbourne's metered taxis are reasonably priced. They require an estimated prepaid fare when hailed between 10pm and 5am.

Melbourne
Neighbourhoods

Carlton & Around (p108)
Home to Melbourne's Italian community, mixed in with students, a literary flavour and some outstanding sights.

◉ Top Sights

Melbourne Museum

Royal Exhibition Building

City Centre (p22)
A lively mix of laneways, cool bars and top-notch restaurants, the city's fashionable streets are balanced with pockets of greenery and the Yarra.

◉ Top Sights

Federation Square

Birrarung Marr

Queen Victoria Market

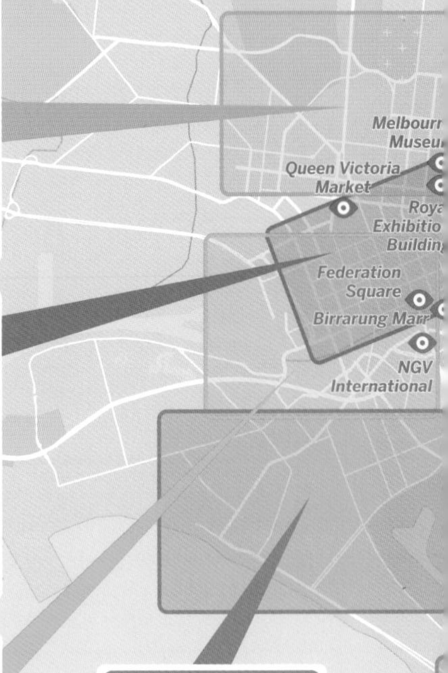

Southbank & Docklands (p46)
Southbank is a slice of European chic along the Yarra. The Docklands is a work in progress, but new eateries make it worth exploring.

◉ Top Sights

NGV International

South Melbourne, Port Melbourne & Albert Park (p58)
Bayside suburbs with a community proud of their local businesses, and the sparkling lake that's home to the Australian Grand Prix.

Melbourne Museum

Queen Victoria Market

Royal Exhibition Building

Federation Square

Birrarung Marr

NGV International

Fitzroy & Collingwood (p92)
These cool-kid inner-city suburbs are full of happening bars, grungy band venues, designer shops, food vans and single-origin-coffee cafes.

Worth a Trip
👁 **Top Sights**
Abbotsford Convent & Around

Abbotsford Convent & Around 👁

East Melbourne & Richmond (p80)
Punt Rd divides genteel East Melbourne and multicultural Richmond. This area is also Melbourne's sporting heartland.

👁 **Top Sights**
Melbourne Cricket Ground

Melbourne Cricket Ground 👁

Royal Botanic Gardens 👁

South Yarra, Prahran & Windsor (p66)
These suburbs are known for shopping – both labels and vintage – and posh South Yarra restaurants plus hipster Windsor hangouts.

👁 **Top Sights**
Royal Botanic Gardens

St Kilda Foreshore

St Kilda (p122)
Bohemian beachside suburb featuring a cast of characters from all walks of life, with a seedy history resisting gentrification.

👁 **Top Sights**
St Kilda Foreshore

Explore
Melbourne

View of the city centre from across the Yarra River
ANDREW WATSON /GETTY IMAGES ©

Explore

City Centre

With the arrival of stylish restaurants, cool laneway bars and boutique shops, the past decade has seen Melbourne's city centre emerge as *the* place to be. At its heart, Federation Square provides the nucleus for the bluestone laneways, arcades, galleries and cosmopolitan streets, all set against a backdrop of the Yarra River and attractive gold-rush-era architecture.

The Sights in a Day

☀ Start the day on ultra-trendy Flinders Lane, treating yourself to one of the city's finest breakfasts at **Cumulus Inc** (p38), before wandering Melbourne's laneways. Check out the world-class street-art scene of edgy stencils and graffiti along **Hosier Lane** (p34) and browse boutique shops such as **Craft Victoria** (p43).

☼ Grab authentic tapas from critically acclaimed **MoVida** (p38), before crossing the road to **Federation Square** (p24) – Melbourne's architecturally arresting centrepiece. Within its precinct don't miss the **Ian Potter Centre: NGV Australia** (p25), home to Indigenous art and Australian modernist paintings. Leave time for **ACMI** (p25) and its multimedia exhibits, and for a stroll through the adjoining parkland of **Birrarung Marr** (p26). Do a hook-turn back to the city's centre to quench a well-earned thirst at **Young & Jackson's** (p37), Melbourne's oldest pub.

☽ Dine on Mexican street food at snazzy **Mamasita** (p38) or old-school Italian at the **Waiters Restaurant** (p39). Grab a pre-show cocktail at **Bar Americano** (p41), before enjoying a night of high culture at the **Opera** (p42) or a rockin' evening at **Cherry** (p31) on ACDC Lane.

For a local's day in the City Centre, see p30.

 Top Sights

 Local Life

 Best of Melbourne

Getting There

🚆 **Train** Iconic Flinders St Station is the main terminal for inner-city and suburban trains, linked via the City Loop to Flagstaff, Melbourne Central, Parliament and Southern Cross.

🚊 **Tram** The city is a hub for Melbourne's trams, which criss-cross its length and travel into the suburbs.

Top Sights
Federation Square

While it's taken some time, Melburnians have finally come to embrace Federation Square, accepting it as the congregation place it was meant to be – somewhere to celebrate, protest, watch major sporting events or hang out on its deckchairs. Occupying a prominent city block, 'Fed Sq' is far from square: its undulating and patterned forecourt is paved with 460,000 hand-laid cobblestones from the Kimberley region, with sight lines to Melbourne's iconic landmarks, and its buildings are clad in a fractal-patterned reptilian skin.

👁 Map p32, E5

www.fedsquare.com.au

cnr Flinders & Swanston Sts

🚊 1, 3, 5, 6, 8, 16, 64, 67, 72, 🚉 Flinders St

Don't Miss

Ian Potter Centre: NGV Australia

Hidden away in the basement of Federation Square, the **Ian Potter Centre** (☎03-8620 2222; www.ngv.vic.gov.au; exhibition costs vary; ☉10am-5pm Tue-Sun) showcases an impressive collection of Australian works. Set over three levels, it's a mix of permanent (free) and temporary (ticketed) exhibitions, comprising paintings, decorative arts, photography, prints, sculpture and fashion. Highlights include the stunning Aboriginal permanent exhibition, colonial artist Tom Roberts' *Shearing the Rams,* modernist 'Angry Penguins' painters Sir Sidney Nolan and Albert Tucker, plus Fred Williams, John Brack and Howard Arkley.

Australian Centre for the Moving Image (ACMI)

Managing to educate, enthrall and entertain in equal parts, **ACMI** (☎03-8663 2200; www.acmi. net.au; admission free; ☉10am-6pm) is a visual feast that pays homage to Australian cinema and TV. It offers insight into the modern-day Australian psyche, perhaps like no other museum can. Its floating screens don't discriminate against age, with TV shows, games and movies on-call for all. It's a great place to waste a day watching TV and not feel guilty about it.

Fed Square Tours

Highly recommended (and free) tours depart from Monday to Saturday at 11am. Tours take in the intricacies of Fed Sq's architecture and design, as well as some interesting Melbourne facts. Spots are limited, so arrive 10 minutes early.

☑ Top Tips

▶ Free tours of the Ian Potter Centre: NGV Australia are conducted daily at 11am, noon, 1pm and 2pm; free tours of ACMI are at 11am and 2.30pm daily.

▶ Get here early for free daily tai chi from 7.30am, or try meditation at 12.30pm each Tuesday.

▶ Grab one of the free deckchairs. Bring a hat and sunscreen; there's no shade outside.

▶ The square has free wi-fi, and mobile phone chargers are provided in the visitor centre.

✗ Take a Break

Over the road, historic Young & Jackson's (p37) has served up beer since 1861. Lounge on chesterfields in Chloe's Bar or head up to the rooftop for Australian ciders on tap. Fed Sq itself has plenty of bars and restaurants; **Transport** (☎03-9658 8808; www.transportpublicbar.com.au; ☉11am-late) is popular for people- and river-watching.

Top Sights
Birrarung Marr

The three-terraced Birrarung Marr is a welcome addition to Melbourne's patchwork of parks and gardens. It features grassy knolls, river promenades, a thoughtful planting of indigenous flora, and great viewpoints of the city and the Yarra River. As a sign of respect to the Wurundjeri people, the traditional owners of the area, Birrarung Marr ('River of Mists') features a snaking eel path with Indigenous Australian art, a shield-and-spear sculpture and an audio installation outside ArtPlay telling the story of contemporary Wurundjeri people.

👁 Map p32, F5

btwn Federation Sq & the Yarra River

🚋 1, 3, 5, 6, 8, 16, 64, 67, 72, 🚆 Flinders St

Deborah Halpern's *Angel* (1988)

Don't Miss

Federation Bells

The sculptural **Federation Bells** (www.federation-bells.com.au; ☉bells 8.30-9.30am, noon-1pm & 5-6pm) perch on the park's upper level and ring out daily like a robotic orchestra. There are 39 computer-controlled brass bells of various sizes and shapes, all with impressive acoustics, playing specially commissioned contemporary compositions.

Angel

Relocated from outside NGV International, the 10m-high, three-legged mosaic *Angel* is a vivid abstract sculpture by artist Deborah Halpern that resembles a dinosaur.

Speakers Corner

In the southeast corner of Birrarung Marr you'll find the original mounds used as soapboxes in the early 20th century. This was also used as a site for demonstrations, including when 50,000 people protested conscription during WWI. Near to here is a dried riverbed lined with ghost gums and palms, creating a tranquil billabong feel.

ArtPlay

Within an old railway building, **ArtPlay** (☏03-9664 7900; www.artplay.com.au; ☉10am-4pm Wed-Sun) hosts creative workshops for two- to 13-year-olds, getting them sewing, singing, painting and puppeteering, and has a cool playground out back.

William Barak Bridge

Stroll over the 'singing' William Barak Bridge (named after the Wurundjeri leader), which provides a scenic route to the MCG accompanied with sound installations. Listen out for songs, words and sounds representing Melbourne's cultural diversity as you walk.

☑ Top Tips

▶ Get online at www.federationbells.com.au to create your own composition to be played at the Federation Bells.

▶ Look out for photo ops, with each of the three terraces providing sight lines to the city's most famous landmarks.

▶ It's one of the best spots in the city to bring the kids, for both ArtPlay and its adventure playground.

✕ Take a Break

The bluestone bar Riverland (p42) overlooking the Yarra River is an atmospheric spot to enjoy a hearty breakfast, lunchtime feed of Mod Oz pub food and, of course, a cold beer.

There are public barbecues along the banks of the Yarra, which are the perfect lunch spot for a sausage sizzle when the sun's out.

Top Sights
Queen Victoria Market

Home to more than 600 traders, the Vic Market is the largest open-air market in the southern hemisphere and attracts thousands of shoppers. It's where Melburnians sniff out fresh produce among the booming cries of spruiking fishmongers and fruit-and-veg vendors. The wonderful deli hall (with art deco features) is lined with everything from soft cheeses, wines and Polish sausages to Greek dips and truffle oil. The Summer Night Market is when it's most buzzing, and packed with punters enjoying a balmy evening of street food.

Map p32, D1

www.qvm.com.au

513 Elizabeth St

6am-2pm Tue & Thu, to 5pm Fri, to 3pm Sat, 9am-4pm Sun

Tourist Shuttle, 19, 55, 57, 59

Don't Miss

Produce
Saturday mornings are particularly buzzing, as marketgoers breakfast to the sounds of buskers. Clothing and knick-knack stalls dominate on Sundays; they're big on variety, but don't come looking for style. (If you're after sheepskin moccasins or cheap T-shirts, you're in luck.)

Evening Markets
Wednesday evenings from mid-November to the end of February the Summer Night Market takes over. It's a lively social event featuring hawker-style food stalls, bars and entertainment. There's a winter version each Wednesday evening in July and August.

History
The market has been on this site for more than 130 years; before that, from 1837 to 1854, the old Melbourne Cemetery stood here. Remarkably, around 9000 bodies remain buried here, from underneath Shed F to the carpark leading to Franklin St. There's a small memorial on the corner of Queen and Therry Sts. Enquire online about Heritage & Cultural Tours.

Street Art
Hidden in an unsigned laneway off Franklin St en route to the market, **Blender Lane** features some of Melbourne's best street art. You'll also find the **Blender Studios** (☑03-9328 5556; www.theblenderstudios.com; 110 Franklin St) and **Dark Horse Experiment** (☑03-9328 5556; www.darkhorseexperiment.com; 110 Franklin St; ⊘noon-6pm Wed-Sat) galleries in an old warehouse-turned-art-studio used by underground artists.

☑ Top Tips

▶ Heritage, cultural and foodie tours run from the market; check online for details.

▶ Grab an Australiana souvenir such as Ugg boots and Driza-Bone coats.

✕ Take a Break

The deli hall and fresh produce stalls have plenty of gourmet and organic goods for a picnic hamper. Choose from glistening olives, soft cheeses and local specialities of kangaroo biltong and regional Victorian wines. Head to nearby Flagstaff Gardens, or Botanic Gardens further afield, to enjoy.

From borek to bratwurst, cheap freshly cooked snacks abound.

Grab an artisan coffee from **Padre Coffee** (String Bean Alley, M Shed near Peel St; ⊘7am-2pm Tue & Thu, to 4pm Fri-Sun; ☒55), which roasts its own beans sourced directly from Africa and South America.

Local Life
Arcades & Laneways

Central Melbourne is a warren of 19th-century arcades and gritty-turned-hip cobbled bluestone laneways featuring fantastic street art, basement restaurants, boutiques and cool dive bars. While the laneways are a celebration of edgy chic, the arcades are gleaming reminders of the grand sophistication that was 19th-century 'Marvellous Melbourne' during the city's gold-rush boom years.

❶ Campbell Arcade

Start underground at pink retro-tiled Campbell Arcade, also known as Degraves Subway. Built for the 1956 Olympics, it's home to a great collection of indie stores. **Sticky** (☏ 03-9654 8559; www.stickyinstitute.com; Shop 10, Campbell Arcade, Flinders St Station; ⏱ noon-6pm Mon-Fri, to 5pm Sat; ℝ Flinders St) is a favourite haunt for those wanting to avoid mainstream press and pick up some hand-photocopied zines.

❷ Degraves St

Degraves St is a sophisticated laneway with boutiques and Parisian-style cafes, including **Degraves Espresso** (⏰7am-9pm Mon-Fri, 8am-9pm Sat, 8am-6pm Sun; 🚋48, 70, 75, 🚉Flinders St), a good spot for a coffee or meal and to soak up the atmosphere.

❸ Centre Place

Centre Place is full of graffiti and cafes, and home to **Hell's Kitchen** (Level 1, 20 Centre Pl; ⏰noon-11pm Mon & Tue, to 1am Wed-Sat, to 10pm Sun; 🚉Flinders St), the original hidden laneway bar. Head up a narrow flight of stairs to sip on classic cocktails and people-watch from the windows. It attracts a young, hip crowd and serves food.

❹ Block Arcade

Built in 1891, Block Arcade features etched-glass ceilings and sparkling mosaic floors that are based on Milan's Galleria Vittorio Emanuele plaza. Venture into **Gewürzhaus** (282 Collins St; 🚋19, 57, 59), a chef's dream stocking spices from around the world, including Indigenous Australian blends, flavoured salts and sugars.

❺ Carson Place

From Little Collins St you'll pass **Dame Edna Place**, named after Moonee Ponds' favourite 'lady', before you reach Carson Place, another quintessential Melbourne lane. The **Butterfly Club** here is an eccentric little cabaret with an extraordinary collection of kitsch; you're never quite sure what you're in for.

❻ Royal Arcade

This Parisian-style shopping arcade was built between 1869 and 1870 and is Melbourne's oldest; the upper walls retain much of the original detail. The black-and-white chequered path leads to the mythological figures of giant brothers Gog and Magog, perched with hammers atop the arched exit to Little Collins St. They've been striking the hour here since 1892.

❼ Rutledge & Hosier Lanes

Next stop is the street-art meccas of Hosier Lane and Rutledge Lane. For the low-down on hidden pieces, sign up with **Melbourne Street Art Tours** (p156), led by street-artist guides.

❽ ACDC Lane & Duckboard Place

Finish down ACDC Lane (named after the band, who are homegrown heroes) at **Cherry** (www.cherrybar.com.au; ACDC Lane; ⏰6pm-3am Tue & Wed, 5pm-5am Thu-Sat, 2-6.30pm Sun; 🚋City Circle, 70, 75), Melbourne's legendary rock 'n' roll bar where a welcoming, slightly anarchic spirit prevails. Live music and DJs play rock 'n' roll seven nights a week, and there's a long-standing soul night on Thursdays. From here, urban Duckboard Pl horseshoes around with more street art.

E **F** **G** **H**

CARLTON

For reviews see

◎ Top Sights	p24
◎ Sights	p34
✖ Eating	p37
☕ Drinking	p41
◆ Entertainment	p42
⊕ Shopping	p43

Bouverie St
Swanston St
Cardigan St
Queensberry St
Drummond St
Rathdowne St

Gertrude St

Victoria St
Melbourne
City Baths

RMIT
University

Old
Melbourne
Gaol

RMIT
University

Mackenzie
St

Russell St

4

Carlton
Gardens
South

FITZROY

La Trobe St

bourne
Central

2 State
◎ Library of
Victoria

⭐ **35**

St Vincent's
Hospital

Fitzroy St

Little Lonsdale St

Jones
La

Spring St

Victoria Pde

Drewery
La

Red Cape La
Artemis La
QV Square

Lonsdale St

Parliament Ⓜ

Parliament
Gardens

Nicholson St

Osborne St

Gisborne St

Albert St

38 ☕**32**
16 ✖

Chinatown ◎**3**

Tattersalls
La

La Trobe
Pl

CHINATOWN

Little Bourke St

⭐**37**
20 Market
33 La

Bourke St

Liverpool
St

Crossley St

8 Parliament
◎ House

St Patrick's
Cathedral

Cathedral Pl

rke St Mall

vellers
Aid

24
☕

Royal La
Russell Pl

☕**30**

Russell St

Little Collins St

Alfred
Pl

Exhibition St

36

Ⓜ

✖**18** Parliament
Meyers
Pl

26

19 ✖
Parliament Ⓜ

Macarthur St

St Andrews Pl

Gordon
Reserve

Swanston St

Town
Hall ⊕**34**

Collins St

Collins
Place

Old Treasury
Building
Treasury Pl

Lansdowne St

Fitzroy
Gardens

City
Square

28
☕

Manchester
La

Hosier
Lane

22 Flinders La
✖

Oliver La

ACDC
La

17 ✖

14✖ ⊕**39**

21 ✖

Spring St

15 ✖

6 ◎

Treasury
Gardens

40 ⊕

10 ◎
Young &
◎ Jackson's

☕**13**

Flinders St

**EAST
MELBOURNE**

ⓘ Melbourne
Visitor Centre

7 ◎

ers
ers ⊕

rs

ders
treet
tion

◎ **Federation
Square**

☕**31**

Princes
Bridge

**Birrarung
Marr** ◎

Batman Ave

Wellington Pde

Wellington Pde S

🧭

0 _____ 400 m
0 _____ 0.25 miles

Sights

Hosier Lane
STREET

1 ⊙ Map p32, E4

Melbourne's most celebrated laneway for street art, Hosier Lane's cobbled length draws camera-wielding crowds snapping edgy graffiti, stencils and art installations. Subject matter runs to the mostly political and countercultural, spiced with irreverent humour; pieces change almost daily (not even a Banksy is safe here). Be sure to check out Rutledge Lane (which horseshoes off Hosier) too. (🚇75, 70)

State Library of Victoria
LIBRARY

2 ⊙ Map p32, E2

A big player in Melbourne's achievement of being named Unesco City of Literature in 2008, the State Library has been the forefront of Melbourne's literary scene since it opened in 1854.

With over two million books in its collection, it's a great place to soak up the atmosphere. Its epicentre, the octagonal **La Trobe Reading Room**, was completed in 1913; its reinforced-concrete dome was the largest of its kind in the world and its natural light illuminates the ornate plasterwork and the studious Melbourne writers who come here to pen their works. Bushranger Ned Kelly's famed armour is housed here too. (📞03-8664 7000; www.slv.vic.gov.au; 328 Swanston St; ⊙10am-9pm Mon-Thu, to 6pm Fri-Sun; 🚋1, 3, 5, 6, 8, 16, 64, 67, 72, 🚉Melbourne Central)

Chinatown
NEIGHBOURHOOD

3 ⊙ Map p32, E3

Chinese miners arrived in search of the 'new gold mountain' in the 1850s and settled in this strip of Little Bourke St, now flanked by traditional red archways. The **Chinese Museum** (📞03-9662 2888; www.chinesemuseum.

Understand
Street Art

Regarded as one of the world's best cities for street art, Melbourne has a painted urban landscape that's a beacon for visitors from all around the world. The myriad laneway walls provide an outdoor canvas for some of the best local and international artists in paste-up, mural and stencil art. Melbourne City Council has embraced the city's 'street art capital of the world' status; artists are invited to do their thing in designated art zones – an irony not lost on the artists, and not something that has stopped stencils gracing unsanctified walls, particularly in the suburbs. These colourful and densely decorated passages include, most famously, Hosier Lane, Blender Lane, Croft Alley, Caledonian Lane and Union Lane.

com.au; 22 Cohen Pl; adult/child $8/6; ⏱10am-5pm) here does a wonderful job of putting it into context with five floors of displays, including artefacts from the gold-rush era, dealings under the xenophobic White Australia policy and the stunning 63m-long, 200kg Millennium Dragon that bends around the building – in full flight it needs eight people just to hold up its head alone. (Little Bourke St, btwn Spring & Swanston Sts; 1, 3, 5, 6, 8, 16, 64, 67, 72)

Old Melbourne Gaol
HISTORIC BUILDING

4 ◉ Map p32, F2

Built in the mid-1800s, this forbidding bluestone prison was in operation until 1929. It's now one of Melbourne's most popular museums, where you can tour the tiny, bleak cells. Around 135 people were hanged here, including Ned Kelly, Australia's most infamous bushranger, in 1880; one of his death masks is on display. (☑03-8663 7228; www.oldmelbournegaol.com.au; 337 Russell St; adult/child/family $25/14/55; ⏱9.30am-5pm; 24, 30, City Circle)

Sea Life Melbourne Aquarium
AQUARIUM

5 ◉ Map p32, B5

This aquarium is home to rays, gropers and sharks, all of which cruise around a 2.2-million-litre tank, watched closely by visitors in a see-through tunnel. See the penguins in icy 'Antarctica' or get up close to one

 Top Tip

City Circle Tram

Catch a free ride on the **City Circle Tram** (Tram 35; ☑13 16 38; www.ptv.vic.gov.au; ⏱10am-6pm Sun-Wed, to 9pm Thu-Sat; 🚊35). The burgundy-coloured tram has recorded commentary and loops along Flinders St, Harbour Esplanade (Docklands), La Trobe and Spring Sts before heading back along Flinders St. It runs every 10 minutes or so between 10am and 6pm (to 9pm Thursday to Saturday during summer), and you can jump on and off at any of the frequent stops.

of Australia's largest saltwater crocs in the crocodile lair. Divers are thrown to the sharks three times a day; for between $210 and $300 you can join them. Admission tickets are cheaper online. (☑03-9923 5999; www.melbourne-aquarium.com.au; cnr Flinders & King Sts; adult/child/family $38/22/93; ⏱9.30am-6pm, last entry 5pm; 🚊70, 75)

Old Treasury Building
MUSEUM

6 Map p32, G4

The fine neoclassical architecture of the Old Treasury (c 1862), designed by JJ Clarke, is a telling mix of hubris and functionality. The basement vaults were built to house the millions of pounds worth of loot that came from the Victorian goldfields and now feature multimedia displays telling stories from the gold rush. Also downstairs is

Flinders Street Station

the charmingly redolent reconstruction of the 1920s caretaker's residence, which beautifully reveals what life in Melbourne was like in the early part of last century. (☎03-9651 2233; www.oldtreasurybuilding.org.au; Spring St; admission free; ⏰10am-4pm, closed Sat; 🚋112, 🚉Parliament)

Flinders Street Station

HISTORIC BUILDING

7 ◉ Map p32, E5

If ever there was a true symbol of the city, Flinders Street Station would have to be it. Built in 1854, it was Melbourne's first railway station, and you'd be hard-pressed to find a Melburnian who hasn't uttered the phrase 'Meet me under the clocks' at one time

or another (the popular rendezvous spot is located at the front entrance of the station). Stretching along the Yarra, it's a beautiful neoclassical building topped with a striking octagonal dome. (cnr Flinders & Swanston Sts)

Parliament House

HISTORIC BUILDING

8 ◉ Map p32, G3

The grand steps of Victoria's parliament (c 1856) are often dotted with slow-moving, tulle-wearing brides smiling for the camera, or placard-holding protesters doing the same. The only way to visit inside is on a tour, where you'll see exuberant use of ornamental plasterwork, stencilling and gilt full of gold-rush-era pride and optimism. Building began with the two main chambers: the lower house (now the legislative assembly) and the upper house (now the legislative council). (☏03-9651 8568; www.parliament.vic.gov.au; Spring St; ⏱tours 9.30am, 10.30am, 11.30am, 1.30pm, 2.30pm & 3.45pm Mon-Fri; 🚋City Circle, 86, 96, 🚉Parliament)

Flagstaff Gardens   PARK

9 ◉ Map p32, C2

Originally known as Burial Hill, these gardens were the site of Melbourne's first cemetery, where eight of the city's early settlers were buried. Today its pleasant open lawns are popular with workers taking a lunchtime break. The gardens contain trees that are well over 100 years old, including Moreton Bay fig trees and a variety of eucalypts, including spotted, sugar and river red gums. There are plenty of possums about, but don't feed them. (William St, btwn La Trobe, Dudley & King Sts; 🚌Tourist Shuttle, 🚋City Circle, 24, 30, 55, 🚉Flagstaff)

Young & Jackson's   HISTORIC BUILDING

10 ◉ Map p32, E5

Across from Flinders Street Station is a pub known less for its beer (served up since 1861) than its iconic nude painting of the teenaged *Chloe*, painted by Jules Joseph Lefebvre. Chloe's yearning gaze, cast over her shoulder and out of the frame, was a hit at the Paris Salon of 1875. (www.youngandjacksons.com.au; cnr Flinders & Swanston Sts; ⏱11am-late; 🚌Tourist

Shuttle, 🚋City Circle, 1, 3, 5, 6, 8, 16, 64, 67, 72, 🚉Flinders St)

Koorie Heritage Trust   CULTURAL CENTRE

11 ◉ Map p32, B2

Devoted to southeastern Aboriginal culture, this cultural centre displays interesting artefacts and oral history. Its gallery spaces show a variety of contemporary and traditional work, with a model scar tree at the centre's heart, and a permanent chronological display of Victorian Koorie history. Behind the scenes, significant objects are carefully preserved; replicas that can be touched by visitors are used in the displays. It's in the process of relocating, so check the website for details. (☏03-8622 2600; www.koorieheritagetrust.com; 295 King St; gold-coin donation, tours $15; ⏱9am-5pm Mon-Fri; 🚋24, 30, 🚉Flagstaff)

Eating

Vue de Monde   MODERN AUSTRALIAN $$$

12 ✗ Map p32, B4

Sitting pretty in the old observation deck of the Rialto, Melbourne's favoured spot for occasion dining has views to match its name. Visionary chef Shannon Bennett has moved away from its classic French style to a subtle Modern Australian theme that runs through everything from the decor to the menu. (☏03-9691 3888; www.vuedemonde.com.au; Rialto, 525 Collins St;

degustation menu $200-250; ⊘reservations from noon-2pm Tue-Fri & Sun, 6-9.15pm Mon-Sat; 🚊11, 31, 48, 109, 112, 🚇Southern Cross)

MoVida
SPANISH $$

13 Map p32, E5

MoVida sits in a cobbled laneway emblazoned with one of the world's densest collections of street art – it doesn't get much more Melbourne than this. Line up along the bar, cluster around little window tables or, if you've booked, take a table in the dining area for fantastic Spanish tapas and *raciones*. (☏03-9663 3038; www.movida. com.au; 1 Hosier Lane; tapas $4-6, raciones $8-28; ⊘noon-late; 🚊70, 75, 🚇Flinders St)

Cumulus Inc
MODERN AUSTRALIAN $$

14 Map p32, G4

One of Melbourne's best for any meal, Cumulus Inc gives you that wonderful Andrew McConnell style along

Top Tip
No Reservations

Many of the city's hottest restaurants (Cumulus Inc, Mamasita and Chin Chin, to name a few) have a 'no bookings' policy, so it's a good idea to arrive early. Most places will take your phone number and call you when a table is free, so you're not awkwardly hanging around waiting. Another option is to take a drink at the bar or a predinner stroll part of your night out.

with reasonable prices. The focus is on beautiful produce and simple but artful cooking: from breakfasts of sardines and smoked tomato on toast at the marble bar to suppers of freshly shucked *clair de lune* oysters tucked away on the leather banquettes. No reservations, so queues are highly probable. (www.cumulusinc.com.au; 45 Flinders Lane; mains $21-38; ⊘7am-11pm Mon-Fri, 8am-11pm Sat & Sun; 🚊City Circle, 48)

Mamasita
MEXICAN $$

15 Map p32, G4

The restaurant responsible for kicking off Melbourne's obsession with authentic Mexican street food, Mamasita is still one of the very best – as evidenced by the perpetual queues to get into the place. The chargrilled corn sprinkled with cheese and chipotle mayo is a legendary starter, and there's a fantastic range of corn-tortilla tacos and 180 types of tequila. No reservations, so prepare to wait. (☏03-9650 3821; www.mamasita.com.au; 1/11 Collins St; tacos from $5, shared plates from $19; ⊘noon-late Mon-Sat, from 1pm Sun; 🚊City Circle, 11, 31, 48, 112)

Cookie
THAI, BAR $$

16 Map p32, E3

Part Thai restaurant, part swanky bar, Cookie does both exceptionally well. Its all-Thai kitchen fires up authentic flavours with fusion twists to create some of the best Thai food in town. The bar is unbelievably well stocked with fine whiskies, wines and craft beers, and

knows how to make a serious cocktail. (03-9663 7660; www.cookie.net.au; 1st fl, Curin House, 252 Swanston St; mains from $17.50; noon-late; 3, 5, 6, 16, 64, 67, 72)

Chin Chin ASIAN $$

 17 Map p32, F4

A great option on Flinders Lane, Chin Chin does delicious Southeast Asian hawker-style food designed as shared plates. It's inside a busied-up shell of an old building with a real New York feel, and while there are no bookings, Go Go Bar downstairs will have you till there's space. (03-8663 2000; www.chinchinrestaurant.com.au; 125 Flinders Lane; mains $19-33; 11am-late; City Circle, 70, 75)

Waiters Restaurant ITALIAN $$

18 Map p32, G4

Head down a laneway and up some stairs to step into this restaurant – and into another era. Opened in 1947, it still bears 1950s drapes, wood panelling and Laminex tables. Once only for Italian and Spanish waiters to unwind after work over a game of *scopa* (a card game), now everyone is welcome for its delicious, hearty plates of red-sauce pasta. (03-9650 1508; 1st fl, 20 Meyers Pl; mains $15-25; noon-2.30pm Mon-Fri & 6pm-late Mon-Sat; Parliament)

Bar Lourinhã TAPAS $$

 19 Map p32, G4

Matt McConnell's wonderful northern Spanish–Portuguese specialities have the swagger and honesty of an Iberian

Bar Lourinhã

shepherd, but with a cluey, metropolitan touch. Start with the zingy kingfish pancetta and finish with the hearty house-made chorizo or baked *morcilla* (blood sausage). There's an intriguing wine list sourced from the region, too. Bookings only for lunch. (03-9663 7890; www.barlourinha.com.au; 37 Little Collins St; tapas $4-24; noon-11pm Mon-Thu, noon-1am Fri, 4pm-1am Sat; Parliament)

Flower Drum CHINESE $$$

 20 Map p32, F3

The Flower Drum continues to be Melbourne's most celebrated Chinese restaurant. The finest, freshest produce prepared with absolute attention

JAMES BRAUND / GETTY IMAGES ©

to detail keeps this Chinatown institution booked out for weeks in advance. The sumptuous, but ostensibly simple, Cantonese food (from a menu that changes daily) is delivered with the slick service you'd expect in such elegant surrounds. (⌀03-9662 3655; www.flower-drum.com; 17 Market Lane; mains $35-55; ⏱noon-3pm & 6-11pm Mon-Sat, 6-10.30pm Sun; 🔊; ▣86, 96)

Gazi

GREEK **$$**

21 Map p32, F5

The lastest offering from George Calombaris of *MasterChef* fame, this rebadged side project to the fancier Press Club (next door) is set in a cavernous industrial space with a menu inspired by Greek street food. Select

from authentic shared starters, gourmet mini souvlakis filled with prawn or duck and wood-fire spit mains. He also owns the East Brunswick eatery Hellenic Republic. (⌀03-9207 7444; www.gazirestaurant.com.au; 2 Exhibition St; shared plates from $10, mains $23; ⏱11.30am-11pm; ▣48, 70, 75)

Coda

MODERN AUSTRALIAN **$$$**

22 Map p32, F4

Coda has a wonderful 'basement' ambience, with exposed lightbulbs and industrial factory-style windows. Its innovative dishes make up an eclectic menu of Asian, French and Modern Australian influences. It's a little hit and miss; some taste plates scream 'yes!', such as crispy prawn and tapioca betel leaf, but others don't quite hit those highs. (⌀03-9650 3155; www.codarestaurant.com.au; basement, 141 Flinders Lane; mains $36-38; ⏱noon-3pm & 6pm-late; ▣11, 31, 48, 86, 112)

Hopetoun Tea Rooms

TEAROOM **$$**

23 Map p32, D4

Since 1892 patrons have been nibbling pinwheel sandwiches here, taking tea (with pinkies raised) and delicately polishing off a lamington. Hopetoun's venerable status has queues almost stretching out the entrance of Block Arcade. Salivate over the window display while you wait. (⌀03-9650 2777; www.hopetountearooms.com.au; 282 Collins St; dishes $13-21; ⏱8am-5pm)

Local Life

Camy Dumplings

It's a Melbourne institution, but there's nothing fancy about **Camy Shanghai Dumpling Restaurant** (Map p32, E3; 23-25 Tattersalls Lane; dumplings 10/20 pieces $5/7; ⏱11.30am-3.30pm & 5-10pm Mon-Fri, noon-10pm Sat, noon-9pm Sun; ▣3, 5, 6, 16, 64, 67, 72). Pour your own plastic cup of tea from the urn, then try a variety of dumplings (steamed or fried) with some greens and BYO booze. Put up with the dismal service and you've found one of the last places in town where you can fill up for under $10.

Drinking

Bar Americano COCKTAIL BAR

24 Map p32, E4

A hideaway bar in a city alleyway, Bar Americano is a standing-room-only affair with black-and-white chequered floors complemented with classic 'do not spit' subway tiled walls and a subtle air of speakeasy. By day it serves excellent coffee but after dark it's all about the cocktails; they don't come cheap but they do come superb. (www.baramericano.com; 20 Pesgrave Pl, off Howey Pl; ⏰8.30am-1am; 🚃11, 31, 109, 112)

Lui Bar COCKTAIL BAR

25 Map p32, B4

One of the city's most sophisticated bars, Lui offers the chance to sample the excellent bar snacks of Vue de Monde. Suits and jet-setters cram in most nights so get there early, claim your table and order drinks from the 'pop-up book' menu containing serious drinks like macadamia martinis – vacuum distilled at the bar. (www.vuedemonde.com.au; Level 55, Rialto, 525 Collins St; ⏰5.30pm-midnight Mon, noon-midnight Tue-Fri, 5.30pm-late Sat, noon-evening Sun; 🚃11, 31, 48, 109, 112, 🚆Southern Cross)

Madame Brussels BAR

26 Map p32, G3

Although named for a famous 19th-century brothel owner, it feels like a camp '60s rabbit hole you've fallen into, with much Astroturfery and staff dressed à la the country club. It's just the tonic to escape the city for a jug of its Madame Brussels–style Pimms on the wonderful rooftop terrace. (www.madamebrussels.com; Level 3, 59-63 Bourke St; ⏰noon-1am; 🚃86, 96)

Chuckle Park BAR

27 Map p32, D4

Chuckle Park uses a healthy dose of Astroturf to park its '70s caravan bar on in the narrowest of laneways. Hanging plant jars double as swaying lights and indie and rock music create the scene while the 'in the know' crowd munch on pulled-pork rolls and share huge jars of cocktails. (www.chucklepark.com.au; 322 Little Collins St; ⏰noon-1am; 🚃86, 96)

Shebeen BAR

28 Map p32, E4

Corrugated iron walls and awnings give this relaxed bar a canteen shack feel. Shebeen (the name for illegal drinking bars in apartheid South Africa) offers a place to have a guilt-free tipple – 100% of drink profits go towards an overseas charity partner. At the time of research there were plans for live music and DJs. (www.shebeen.com.au; 36 Manchester Lane; ⏰11am-late Mon-Fri, 4pm-late Sat, 4-11pm Sun; 🚃11, 31, 48, 109, 112)

Brother Baba Budan CAFE

29 Map p32, D3

This small city cafe by Seven Seeds, with just a few seats (most hangin' from the ceiling), does a roaring takeaway coffee trade for the inner-city workers and is a great spot for a mid-shopping caffeine buzz. Don't be put off by queues; service is fast and friendly. (www.sevenseeds.com.au; 359 Little Bourke St; ⏱7am-5pm Mon-Sat, 9am-5pm Sun; 📶; 🚋19, 57, 59)

Carlton Hotel   BAR

30 🍸 Map p32, E4

Over-the-top Melbourne rococo gets another workout here and never fails to raise a smile. Check out the Palmz rooftop bar if you're looking for some Miami-flavoured vice, or just a great view. (www.thecarlton.com.au; 193 Bourke St; ⏱4pm-late; 🚋86, 96)

Riverland   BAR

31 🍸 Map p32, E5

Perched below Princes Bridge alongside the Yarra River, this bluestone beauty keeps things simple with good wine, beer on tap and bar snacks that hit the mark: charcuterie, cheese and BBQ sausages. Outside tables are a treat when the weather is kind. Be prepared for rowdiness pre- and post-footy matches at the nearby MCG. (📞03-9662 1771; www.riverlandbar.com; Vaults 1-9 Federation Wharf, under Princes Bridge; ⏱10am-late Mon-Fri, 9am-late Sat & Sun; 🚆Flinders St)

Section 8   BAR

32 🍸 Map p32, E3

Enclosed within a cage full of shipping containers and wooden-pallet seating, Section 8 remains one of the city's hippest bars. It does great hot dogs,

including vegan ones. (www.section8.com.au; 27-29 Tattersalls Lane; ⏱10am-late Mon-Fri, noon-late Sat & Sun; 🚋3, 5, 6, 16, 64, 67, 72)

Croft Institute   BAR

33 🍸 Map p32, F3

Hidden in a laneway off a laneway with great grafitti, the slightly creepy Croft is a laboratory-themed bar downstairs, while upstairs on weekends it opens up the 1950s-themed gymnasium bar. There's a $10 cover charge for DJs Friday and Saturday nights. (📞03-9671 4399; www.thecroft-institute.com; 21-25 Croft Alley; ⏱5pm-1am Mon-Thu, to 3am Fri & Sat; 🚋86, 96)

Entertainment

Melbourne Opera   OPERA

34 ⭐ Map p32, E4

A not-for-profit company that performs a classic repertoire in the stunning **Athenaeum** (📞03-9650 1500; www.athenaeumtheatre.com.au; 188 Collins St; 🚋11, 31, 48, 112). Prices are deliberately kept affordable. (📞03-9614 4188; www.melbourneopera.com)

Bennetts Lane   JAZZ

35 ⭐ Map p32, F2

Bennetts Lane has long been the boiler room of Melbourne jazz. It attracts the cream of local and international talent and an audience that knows when it's time to applaud a solo. Beyond the cosy front bar, there's another space reserved for big gigs. (📞03-9663 2856; www.bennettslane.com; 25 Bennetts Lane; ⏱9pm-late; 🚋City Circle, 24, 30)

Boney LIVE MUSIC, BAR

36 Map p32, F4

Taking over from one of Melbourne's most infamous rock 'n' roll bars (called Pony), this new version may be more sanitised, but the good news is it's still got the late-night 2am gigs upstairs, covering anything from fuzzed-out garage to electronica. Its American-diner-meets-Thai food is fantastic, too. (📞03-9663 8268; www.boney.net.au; 68 Little Collins St; ⏱noon-3am Mon-Wed, to 5am Thu, to 7am Fri & Sat; 🚋86, 96, 112)

Ding Dong Lounge LIVE MUSIC

37 Map p32, F3

One of the first venues that made the city cool in the early 2000s, Ding Dong has received a post-modern makeover, but remains one of the city centre's premier rock 'n' roll venues for smaller touring acts and local bands. (📞03-9654 3549; www.dingdong-lounge.com.au; Level 1, 18 Market Lane; ⏱Wed-Sun; 🚋86, 96)

Rooftop Cinema CINEMA

38 Map p32, E3

This rooftop bar sits at dizzying heights on top of the happening Curtain House. In summer it transforms into an outdoor cinema with striped deckchairs and a calendar of new and classic favourite flicks. (www.rooftop-

GPO (p45)

cinema.com.au; Level 6, Curtin House, 252 Swanston St; 🚇Melbourne Central)

Shopping

Craft Victoria Shop CRAFT, DESIGN

39 Map p32, G4

This retail arm of Craft Victoria showcases the best of handmade, mainly by local Victorian artists. Its range of jewellery, textiles, accessories, glass and ceramics bridges the art/craft divide and makes for some wonderful mementos of Melbourne. There are also a few galleries with changing exhibitions; admission is free. (www.craft.org.au; 31 Flinders Lane; ⏱10am-5pm Mon-Sat; 🚋City Circle, 70, 75)

Understand

Indigenous Melbourne

In the Dreaming, the land and the people were created by the spirit Bunjil – 'the great one, old head-man, eagle hawk' – who continues to watch over the Wurundjeri from Tharangalk-bek, the home of the spirits in the sky. The land is entrusted to the people, and they carry a sacred pact to welcome visitors.

The catchment of the Yarra River has been home to the Wurundjeri-willem people for at least 45,000 years. The Wurundjeri were a tribe of the Woiworung, one of five distinct language groups belonging to the Kulin Nation. They often traded and celebrated among the towering red gums, tea trees and ferns of the river's edge with their coastal counterparts the Bunnerong, as well as the clans from the north and west. As the flood-prone rivers and creeks broke their banks in winter, bark shelters would be built north in the ranges. Possums were hunted for their meat and skinned to make calf-length cloaks. Worn with fur against skin, the smooth outer hide was rubbed with waterproofing fat and embellished with totemic designs: graphic chevrons and diamonds or representations of emus and kangaroos.

During the summer, camps were made along the Yarra, the Maribyrnong and Merri Creek. Food was plentiful, and ranged from slow-roasted kangaroo, waterfowl, fish and eel to grubs, yam daisies and banksia-blossom cordial. In 1835, when John Batman arrived from Van Diemen's Land, the Wurundjeri's profound relationship with the land and intimate knowledge of story, ceremony and season would be irrevocably damaged within a few short years. European diseases and a polluted water supply killed many of those who continued to camp by the Yarra.

As the settlement of Melbourne transmogrified from pastoral outpost to heaving gold-rush metropolis in scarcely 30 years, the cumulative effects of dispossession, alcohol and increasing acts of violence saw a decline in Melbourne's Indigenous population. From the earliest days, the colonial authorities evicted Wurundjeri and other Kulin people from their lands, and by the 1870s they were moved on to the four corners of Victoria. Despite this, the Wurundjeri have survived. Melbourne has an Indigenous population of around 15,000, some of whom are of direct Kulin Nation descent. They continue to live, practise and renew their culture to this day.

Alice Euphemia
FASHION, JEWELLERY

40 Map p32, E4

Art-school cheek abounds in the Australian-made and -designed labels sold here – Romance was Born, Karla Spetic and Kloke, to name a few. Jewellery sways between the shocking and exquisitely pretty, and the upstairs space hosts regular events and exhibitions. (Shop 6, Cathedral Arcade, 37 Swanston St; ⊙10am-6pm Mon-Thu & Sat, to 7pm Fri, noon-5pm Sun; ⊠Flinders St)

Somewhere
FASHION, ACCESSORIES

41 Map p32, D4

Somewhere is an apt name for this hard-to-find treasure. It's located at the Little Collins St end of Royal Arcade (look for the Marais sign and take the stairs to level 2). The whitewashed warehouse space stocks predominantly Scandinavian labels, as well as local designers for men and women, along with leather tote bags, Anne Black ceramic jewellery and a good range of denim. (www.someplace.com.au; Royal Arcade, 2/314 Little Collins St; ⊙10am-6pm Mon-Sat, to 8pm Fri, 11am-5pm Sun; ⊠86, 96)

Melbournalia
GIFTS, SOUVENIRS

42 Map p32, G3

Pop-up store turned permanent, this is the place to stock up on interesting souvenirs by local designers – from tram tote bags and city-rooftop honey to prints of the city's icons and great books on Melbourne. (www.melbournalia. com.au; Shop 5, 50 Bourke St; ⊙10am-6pm Mon-Thu, 10am-8pm Fri, 11am-5pm Sat & Sun; ⊠86, 96)

GPO
SHOPPING CENTRE

43 Map p32, D3

This was once simply somewhere you went to buy a stamp, but a postfire restoration made it an atmospheric place to shop. It now houses a three-storey concept store for behemoth H&M. (www. melbournesgpo.com; cnr Elizabeth St & Bourke St Mall; ⊙10am-6pm Mon-Thu & Sat, to 8pm Fri, 11am-5pm Sun; ⊠19, 57, 59, 86, 96)

City Hatters
ACCESSORIES

44 Map p32, E5

Located beside the main entrance to Flinders St Station, this is the most convenient place to purchase an iconic Akubra hat, a kangaroo-leather sun hat or something a little more unique. (www.cityhatters.com.au; 211 Flinders St; ⊙9.30am-6pm Mon-Fri, 9am-5pm Sat, 10am-4pm Sun; ⊠Flinders St)

Claude Maus
FASHION

45 Map p32, E4

Subtly gothic, darkly urban and very Melbourne local label by lapsed artist Rob Maniscalco. You'll find great jeans, textural pieces and leather for men and women in a heritage-listed shop. Other branches at Brunswick St and Swanston St. (www.claudemaus.com; 19 Manchester Lane; ⊙10am-6pm Mon-Sat, to 7pm Fri, 11am-5pm Sun; ⊠Flinders St)

Explore

Southbank & Docklands

Not so long ago a gritty industrial site, Southbank has been reborn as an attractive European-style promenade with restaurants stretching along the Yarra directly across from Flinders St. It's also home to the city's major arts precinct, including galleries, theatres and dance companies. To the city's west lies the Docklands: once working wharves now a mini-city of high-rise apartments and restaurants.

The Sights in a Day

☀ Get your bearings atop the **Melbourne Star** (p51) observation wheel, looking over the city and beyond. Once back on ground, browse the Dockland's precinct of restaurants, before jumping on the free **City Circle Tram** (p35) to scuttle over the river to another emerging waterfront development along South Wharf. Grab lunch and a drink at one of many funky new places along the river, either **Bangpop** (p53) for Thai or the open-air **Boatbuilders Yard** (p54) for barbecue and beer.

☀ Stroll along the river en route to picturesque Southbank. Enjoy dazzling city views, best taken from atop **Eureka Skydeck** (p51). Make your way up St Kilda Rd to see masterpieces by Picasso and the Impressionists at **NGV International** (p48). Afterwards, drop into the box office at the **Arts Centre** (p52) to see what shows take your fancy.

☾ At sunset head back along the Yarra for a wine at **Ponyfish Island** (p53), which perches under a bridge. After drinking up an appetite, make your way to Crown Casino for its upmarket restaurants, which you're best advised to book a day or two in advance. In the evening, catch a show at the Arts Centre, enjoy a night at the casino, or wander the promenade and watch quality street performers along Southbank.

 Top Sights

NGV International (p48)

💗 **Best of Melbourne**

Drinking

Ponyfish Island (p53)

Boatbuilders Yard (p54)

Entertainment

Malthouse Theatre (p54)

Chunky Move (p54)

Getting There

Southbank

🚃 **Train** Flinders St Station

🚃 **Tram** 1, 3, 5, 6, 8, 16, 64, 67, 72

Docklands

🚃 **Train** Southern Cross Station

🚃 **Tram** 30, 35, 48, 70, 75, 86, 96, 109, 112

Top Sights
NGV International

Beyond the gallery's iconic water-wall facade you'll find an expansive collection set over four levels, covering international art that runs from the ancient to the contemporary. In addition to the free permanent collection, comprising Asian and Central American art along with Rembrandt, Monet, Turner and Picasso, the international blockbuster shows are also popular. Previous years have brought touring large-scale shows on the Impressionists, Dalí and the Guggenheim collection, which have resulted in queues reaching outside the building and down St Kilda Rd.

👁 Map p50, E3

📞 03-8662 1555

www.ngv.vic.gov.au

180 St Kilda Rd

exhibition costs vary

🕙 10am-5pm Wed-Mon

🚌 Tourist Shuttle, 🚊 1, 3, 5, 6, 8, 16, 64, 67, 72

Don't Miss

Paintings

Key works include a Rembrandt, a Tiepolo and a Bonnard. You might also bump into a Monet, a Modigliani, a Bacon or a Turner. NGV is home to Picasso's *Weeping Woman,* which was the victim of an art heist in 1986. It's also home to Vincent van Gogh's *Head of a Man,* which remains an international source of conjecture over its authenticity.

Asian Art

The gallery boasts an excellent Asian decorative arts collection, with beautiful pieces on display including Tibetan mandalas, Burmese lacquered betel boxes, Chinese porcelain, Japanese pottery and sculptures of Hindu deities.

Antiquities

Artefacts and relics from Ancient Egypt and Greece are on display, as well as Middle Eastern and European items. Central America is also well represented in the Art of Mesoamerica collection comprising 12th-century masks, jewellery and vessels.

Art & Design

NGV has a fantastic modern art and design collection, spanning paintings, sculptures, photography, fashion, textiles and multimedia from the Americas and Europe.

Architecture

Completed in 1967, the NGV building – Roy Grounds' 'cranky icon' – is one of Australia's most originally controversial but ultimately later respected modernist masterpieces. It was designed with a strict geometry and clear circulation patterns, and made extensive use of wood, glass and bluestone.

☑ **Top Tips**

▸ Free 45-minute tours run hourly from 11am to 2pm, each focusing on different parts of the collection.

▸ Most paintings come with detailed captions, so an audioguide isn't essential.

▸ Australian artists are held at the Ian Potter Centre: NGV Australia (p25) at nearby Federation Square.

▸ The museum has free wi-fi.

✕ **Take a Break**

Take a short stroll to Southbank's riverfront promenade and Ponyfish Island (p53), a fantastic hidden nook serving drinks and light bar snacks such as toasted sandwiches.

The gallery's Great Hall has lounges to rest achy legs beneath a sweeping stained-glass ceiling. Otherwise, on sunny days pre-pack a picnic and head to the Domain Gardens across the road.

WEST MELBOURNE

MELBOURNE

SOUTHBANK

DOCKLANDS

SOUTH MELBOURNE

Federation Square

Princes Bridge

St Kilda Rd

Melbourne Recital Centre

Australian Centre for Contemporary Art

CityLink

City Rd

Crown Casino & Entertainment Complex

Melbourne Exhibition Centre

South Wharf

Southbank Promenade

Southbank Blvd

Batman Park

Yarra River

Queensbridge St

Flinders La

Flinders St

Collins La

Collins St

Bourke St

Little Bourke St

Lonsdale St

Little Collins St

La Trobe St

Elizabeth St

William St

King St

Spencer St

Southern Cross (Spencer St)

Flagstaff Gardens

Batman St

Dudley St

Jeffcott St

Adderley St

Wurundjeri Way

Harbour Esp

Docklands Dr

Footscray Rd

Victoria Harbour

Melbourne Star

Melbourne Central

Flagstaff

Docklands Park

North Wharf Rd

Webb Bridge

Charles Grimes Bridge

Yarra River

Lorimer St

West Gate Fwy

Normanby Rd

Brady St

Ingles St

Wells St

Dodds St

Sturt St

Moore St

Power St

Clarendon St

Spencer St Bridge

Whiteman St

Hale St

Market St

Polly Woodside

South Woodside Centre

400 m
0.25 miles

N

Sights

Melbourne Star   FERRIS WHEEL

1  Map p50, A1

Originally erected in 2009, then disassembled due to structural problems before financial issues delayed it for several years more, the Melbourne Star ferris wheel is finally turning. Joining the London Eye and Singapore Flyer, this giant observation wheel has glass cabins that take you up 120m for 360-degree views of the city, Port Phillip Bay and even further afield to Geelong and the Dandenongs. Rides last 30 minutes.

For an extra $8 you can head back for another ride at night to see the bright lights of the city. (☏03-8688 9688; www.melbournestar.com; 101 Waterfront Way, Docklands; adult/child/family $32/19/82; ⏰10am-10pm; 🚊City Circle, 70, 86, 🚃Southern Cross)

Eureka Skydeck   LOOKOUT

2  Map p50, E3

Melbourne's tallest building, the 297m-high Eureka Tower was built in 2006, and an elevator ride takes you to its 88 floors in less than 40 seconds (check out the photo on the elevator floor). The 'Edge' – a slightly sadistic glass cube – cantilevers you out of the building; you've got no choice but to look down. (www.eurekaskydeck.com.au; 7 Riverside Quay, Southbank; adult/child/family $18.50/10/42, The Edge extra $12/8/29; ⏰10am-10pm, last entry 9.30pm; 🚃Tourist Shuttle)

Melbourne Star

Australian Centre for Contemporary Art   GALLERY

3  Map p50, E4

ACCA is one of Australia's most exciting and challenging contemporary galleries, showcasing local and international artists. The building is, fittingly, sculptural, with a rusted exterior evoking the factories that once stood on the site, and a soaring interior designed to house often massive installations. From Flinders St Station, walk across Princes Bridge and along St Kilda Rd. Turn right at Grant St, then left to Sturt. (ACCA; ☏03-9697 9999; www.accaonline.org.au; 111 Sturt St, Southbank; admission free; ⏰10am-5pm Tue & Thu-Sun, 10am-8pm Wed; 🚃1)

Arts Centre Melbourne

ARTS CENTRE

4 Map p50, E3

The Arts Centre is made up of two separate buildings: Hamer Hall (the concert hall) and the theatres building (under the spire). Both are linked by a series of landscaped walkways. The **George Adams Gallery** and **St Kilda Road Foyer Gallery** are free gallery spaces with changing exhibitions. In the foyer of the theatres building, pick up a self-guided booklet for a tour of art commissioned for the building and including works by Arthur Boyd, Sidney Nolan and Jeffrey Smart. (✆bookings 1300 182 183; www.artscentremelbourne.com.au; 100 St Kilda Rd, Southbank; ⏰box office 9am-8.30pm Mon-Fri, 10am-5pm Sat; 🚌Tourist Shuttle, 🚊1, 3, 5, 6, 8, 16, 64, 67, 72, 🚉Flinders St)

Polly Woodside

MUSEUM

5 Map p50, C3

The *Polly Woodside* is a restored iron-hulled merchant ship (or 'tall ship'), dating from 1885, that now rests in a pen off the Yarra River. A glimpse of the rigging makes for a tiny reminder of what the Yarra would have looked like in the 19th century, dense with ships at anchor. (✆03-9699 9760; www.pollywoodside.com.au; 2a Clarendon St, South Wharf; adult/child/family $16/10/43; ⏰10am-4pm Sat & Sun, daily during school holidays; 🚌96, 109, 112)

Melbourne Recital Centre

ARTS CENTRE

6 Map p50, E3

This award-winning (for its acoustics) building may look like a framed piece of giant honeycomb, but it's actually the home (or hive?) of the Melbourne Chamber Orchestra and lots of small ensembles. The program ranges from contemporary performances to classical chamber music and *Babar the Elephant*. From Flinders St Station, cross the Yarra and turn right at Southbank Blvd. (✆03-9699 3333; www.melbournerecital.com.au; cnr Southbank Blvd & Sturt St, Southbank; ⏰box office 9am-5pm Mon-Fri; 🚌Tourist Shuttle, 🚊1)

Understand
Bunjil

As you drive on one of the many roads surrounding the Docklands, or catch a train to or from Southern Cross Station, you can't miss *Eagle*. Let's just say this bird has presence. Local sculptor Bruce Armstrong was inspired by the figure of Bunjil, the Wurundjeri creator spirit. The cast-aluminium bird rests contentedly on a mammoth jarrah perch, confidently surveying all around with a serene, glassy gaze. (Upon its unveiling, one cheeky journalist called the sculpture 'a bulked-up budgerigar'.) He's a reminder of the wordless natural world, scaled to provide a gentle parody of the surrounding cityscape's attempted domination.

Eating

Rockpool Bar & Grill
MODERN AUSTRALIAN $$$

7 Map p50, D3

The Melbourne outpost of Neil Perry's empire offers his signature seafood raw bar, but it's really all about beef, from grass-fed to full-blood wagyu. This darkly masculine space is simple and stylish, as is the menu. The bar offers the same level of food service with the added bonus of a rather spectacular drinks menu. (☎03-8648 1900; www.rockpoolmelbourne.com; Crown Entertainment Complex, Southbank; mains $20-140; ☉lunch Sun-Fri, dinner daily; 🚊55, 96, 109, 112 🚈Flinders St)

Bangpop
THAI $$

8 Map p50, B3

Sitting on the waterfront at South Wharf, Bangpop breathes a bit of colour and vibrancy into the area with its bar made from Lego, suspended bicycles hanging from the ceiling and dangling neon bulbs. Tasty Thai hawker-style dishes are served at communal cafe tables and accompanied by smoked margaritas. (☎03-9245 9800; www.bangpop.com.au; 35 South Wharf Promenade, South Wharf; mains $16-30; ☉noon-10.30pm Sun-Thu, to 11pm Fri & Sat; 🚊City Circle, 70)

Bopha Devi
CAMBODIAN $$

9 Map p50, A2

The modern Cambodian food here is a delightful mix of novel and familiar

 Top Tip

Casino Dining

The Crown Casino complex is packed with eating options, but some are better than others. Our top tips: Neil Perry's Rockpool Bar & Grill, or his **Spice Temple** (☎03-8679 1888; www.spicetemplemelbourne.com; mains $12-45; ☉yum cha noon-3pm Thu-Sun, dinner 6pm-late daily; 🚊55, 96, 109, 112 🚈Flinders St) for delicious à la carte yum cha; global empire **Nobu** (☎03-9292 5777; www.noburestaurants.com; dishes $20-120; ☉noon-2.30pm & 6-10.30pm; 🚊55, 96, 109, 112 🚈Flinders St) for Japanese; or **Atlantic** (☎03-9698 8888; www.theatlantic.com.au; dishes $18-105; ☉noon-3pm & 6-11pm; 🚊55, 96, 109, 112 🚈Flinders St), where you can throw down oysters at the bar.

Southeast Asian flavours and textures. Herb-strewn salads, noodles and soups manage to be both fresh and filling. (☎03-9600 1887; www.bophadevi.com; 27 Rakaia Way, Docklands; mains $18-27; ☉lunch & dinner; 🚊City Circle, 70, 86)

Drinking

Ponyfish Island
CAFE, BAR

10 Map p50, E2

Laneway bars have been done to death, so now Melburnians are finding new creative spots to do their drinkin'. Where better than a little open-air nook under a bridge arcing over the Yarra River. From

Flinders St Station underground passage, head over the pedestrian bridge towards Southgate where you'll find steps down to people knocking back beers with toasted sangas or cheese plates. (www. ponyfish.com.au; under Yarra Pedestrian Bridge, Southbank; ⊘8am-1am; ⍞Flinders St)

Boatbuilders Yard BAR

11 Map p50, B3

Occupying a slice of South Wharf next to the historic *Polly Woodside* ship, Boatbuilders attracts a mixed crowd of office workers, travellers and Melburnians keen to discover this developing area. It's made up of 'zones' running seamlessly from the indoor cafe-bar to the outdoor BBQ and cider garden, bocce pit and soon-to-come summer gelato bar. (✆03-9686 5088; 23 South Wharf Promenade, South Wharf; ⊘7am-late; ⍞City Circle, 70, 71)

Story CAFE

12 Map p50, B2

Another coffee spot from Dukes, this one does a roaring trade for the Docklands office workers, filling the gap for great coffee in the area. It's a short walk from Southern Cross Station along the concourse towards Docklands Stadium. (700 Bourke St, Docklands; ⊘7am-4.30pm Mon-Fri; ⍞Southern Cross)

Alumbra CLUB

13 Map p50, B2

Great music and a stunning location will impress – even if the Bali-meets-Morocco follies of the decor don't. If you're going to do one megaclub in Melbourne (and like the idea of a glass dance floor), this is going to be your best bet. It's in one of the old sheds jutting out into Docklands' Victoria Harbour. (✆03-8623 9666; www.alumbra. com.au; Shed 9, Central Pier, 161 Harbour Esplanade, Docklands; ⊘4pm-3am Fri & Sat, to 1am Sun; ⍞Tourist Shuttle, ⍞City Circle, 70)

Entertainment

Malthouse Theatre THEATRE

14 Map p50, E4

The Malthouse Theatre Company often produces the most exciting theatre in Melbourne. Dedicated to promoting Australian works, the company has been housed in the atmospheric Malthouse Theatre since 1990 (when it was known as the Playbox). From Flinders St Station walk across Princes Bridge and along St Kilda Rd. Turn right at Grant St, then left into Sturt. (✆03-9685 5111; www.malthousetheatre.com.au; 113 Sturt St, Southbank; ⍞1)

Chunky Move DANCE

15 ⭐ Map p50, E4

This partially government-funded contemporary dance company performs internationally acclaimed pop-inspired pieces at its sexy venue behind the Australian Centre for Contemporary Art. It also runs a variety of dance, yoga and Pilates classes; check the website. From Flinders St Station walk across Princes

Bridge and along St Kilda Rd. Turn right at Grant St then left into Sturt. (☎03-9645 5188; www.chunkymove.com; 111 Sturt St, Southbank; 🚋1)

Melbourne Theatre Company

THEATRE

16 ⭐ Map p50, E3

Melbourne's major theatrical company stages around 15 productions each year, ranging from contemporary and modern (including many new Australian works) to Shakespearean and other classics. Performances take place in a brand-new, award-winning venue in Southbank. (MTC; ☎03-8688 0800; www.mtc.com.au; 140 Southbank Blvd, Southbank; 🚋1)

Hamer Hall

CONCERT VENUE

17 ⭐ Map p50, E3

Having recently undergone a multi-million-dollar redevelopment, the concert hall is well known for its acoustics, with a decor inspired by Australia's mineral and gemstone deposits. (Melbourne Concert Hall; ☎1300 182 183; www.artscentremelbourne.com.au; Arts Centre Melbourne, 100 St Kilda Rd, Southbank; 🚋1, 3, 16, 64, 72, 🚆Flinders St)

Melbourne Symphony Orchestra

ORCHESTRA

The MSO has a broad reach: while not afraid to be populist (it's done sell-out performances with both Burt Bacharach and the Whitlams), it can also do edgy – such as performing with Kiss – along with its performances of the great masterworks of symphony. It

performs regularly at venues around the city, including home venue Hamer Hall (see 17 ⭐ Map p50, E3), Melbourne Town Hall and the Recital Centre (p52). Also runs a summer series of free concerts at the Sidney Myer Music Bowl. (MSO; ☎03-9929 9600; www.mso.com.au)

Etihad Stadium

SPORTS STADIUM

18 ⭐ Map p50, B2

Both comfortable and easy to access, this Docklands stadium seats 52,000 for regular AFL games and the odd one-day cricket match and Rugby Union test, with the advantage of a retractable roof to keep spectators dry. Also runs tours for sporting tragics. (☎03-8625 7700, tours 03-8625 7277; www.etihadstadium.com.au; Bourke St, Docklands; tours adult/child/concession/family $15/8/12/39; 🚋70, 75, 86, 96, 109, 112, 🚆Southern Cross)

Shopping

NGV Shop at NGV International

ART

19 🔒 Map p50, E3

Although not of the same calibre as the great museum shops of the world, this stylish retail space offers some well-designed and thoughtful show-based merchandise, specially mixed CDs, an obligatory but beautifully produced range of posters, as well as an erudite collection of books. Also at the Ian Potter Centre: NGV Australia (p25). (☎03-8620 2243; www.ngv.vic.gov.au; 180 St Kilda Rd, Southbank; ⊙10am–5pm Wed-Mon)

Local Life
Williamstown

A trip over the Westgate Bridge brings you to the seaside suburb of Williamstown, a yacht-filled gem with a historic, salty seafaring atmosphere. In what is one of Melbourne's oldest settlements you'll find plenty of charming 19th-century architecture. It has stunning cityscape views of Melbourne best enjoyed by ferry, the most popular and fitting way to arrive, given the area's maritime ambience.

Getting There

⚓ Williamstown Ferries and Melbourne River Cruises arrive at Gem Pier.

🚆 Williamstown line departs from Flinders St.

🚲 Hobsons Bay Coastal Trail links up with the Maribyrnong River Trail via the city.

❶ Scienceworks

One of Melbourne's most popular attractions for families, **Scienceworks** (☎13 11 02; www.museumvictoria.com.au/scienceworks; 2 Booker St, Spotswood; adult/child $10/free, Planetarium & Lightning Room additional adult/child $6/4.50; ⏰10am-4.30pm; ᯮSpotswood) is an interactive museum that's all about pushing buttons and pulling levers, and basically making learning fun. Displays cover the science of sport (you'll get to run against Cathy Freeman) and the human body. The Melbourne Planetarium here recreates the night sky on a 16m-domed ceiling using a high-tech computer and projection system.

❷ Waterfront Promenade

Williamstown's main strip hugs the harbourfront, making it the place to soak up seaside charm. Here you'll find historic shopfronts, bluestone pubs and a park overlooking the bay to eat fish and chips in. Or pop into **Ragusa** (☎03-9399 8500; www.ragusarestaurant.com.au; 139 Nelson Pl; mains $17-34; ⏰noon-3pm & 6pm-late) for modern Croatian set in a heritage building.

❸ Gem Pier

Williamstown's centrepiece is the ferry arrival point, a sparkling marina surrounded by bobbing yachts and sensational city views. The **Hobsons Bay Visitor Information Centre** (☎03-9932 4310; www.visithobsonsbay.com.au; cnr Syme St & Nelson Pl) should be your first stop for free historical walking tours Tuesdays at 2.15pm and Fridays 11.45am,

except winter. Also here is the HMAS *Castlemaine,* a WWII minesweeper.

❹ Customs Wharf Galleria

The historic **Customs Wharf Galleria** (www.customswharf.com.au; 126 Nelson Pl; admission free; ⏰11am-5pm) is worth a look for quality original artwork, mostly by local artists, housed within the attractive former customs house, built in 1875.

❺ Seaworks & Sea Shepherd

The industrial **Seaworks Maritime Precinct** (☎0417 292 021; www.seaworks.com.au; 82 Nelson Pl) has been redeveloped to comprise a maritime museum and headquarters for **Sea Shepherd Australia** (www.seashepherd.org.au). On weekends you can tour anti-poaching vessels from noon to 4.30pm or drop by the centre for displays about its anti-whaling campaign.

❻ Point Gellibrand

The site of Victoria's first white settlement, Point Gellibrand is where Victoria's navy was established, and where the Timeball Tower, once used by ships to set their chronometers, was built by convict labour in 1840.

❼ Williamstown Beach

Williamstown Beach comprises a soft sweep of sand and picturesque bay waters. Swim in nice weather, or take a coastal walk from Point Gellibrand for wonderful city views. Backing on to the beach, the botanic gardens were established in 1860.

Explore

South Melbourne, Port Melbourne & Albert Park

There's something boastful about these upmarket suburbs, which include some of Melbourne's watery highlights: the bay, the beach and expansive Albert Park Lake. Proud residents reside in single-fronted Victorian and Federation homes, rejoicing in their peaceful environment (except during the Grand Prix). The South Melbourne Market is where you'll find boutique homewares, top cafes and gastropubs.

HARJONO DJOYOBISONO / ALAMY ©

The Sights in a Day

☀ Set off midmorning to **South Melbourne Market** (p62) and grab a coffee at **Clement** (p64) or **Padre Coffee** (p64) – and a sneaky dim sim, an institution here. Then work it off with a stroll around the picturesque streets and over to **Station Pier** (p62) in Port Melbourne to observe the harbour activity and maybe even take a brisk swim at one of the city bay beaches.

☼ Make your way to **Albert Park Lake** (p62) for more exercise walking around the Formula One street circuit. Then shop at the boutique stores, and sample a classic Australian-style burger with the lot at **Andrew's** (p64). Go for a coffee at **Mart 130** (p64), a unique tram-stop cafe. Have a walk around **Gasworks Arts Park** (p62), taking in the galleries and open-air sculptures, and be sure to make time for beer tasting at **Matilda Bay Brewery** (p65).

☾ Let evening drinks and dinner merge into one at friendly local watering hole **Albert Park Hotel** (p63), great for regional beers and a seafood meal. Follow it up with ice cream from nearby **Jock's** (p64) for dessert. Head back to Gasworks for quality independent theatre, or the open-air cinema during summer.

 Best of Melbourne

Cafes
St Ali (p63)

Mart 130 (p64)

Eating
Albert Park Hotel Oyster Bar & Grill (p63)

Andrew's Burgers (p64)

Getting There
🚃 **Tram** 1, 96, 109, 112.

A   B   C   D

1

Bertie St
Fennell St
Ingles St
Woodruff St
Bridge St
Plummer St
Graham St
White St
Boundary St
Munro St
Normanby Rd
Woodgate St
Gladstone St
Montague St
Buckhurst St
Boundary St
Port Melbourne Cricket Ground

12

2

Williamstown Rd
Derham St
Little Derham St
Evans St
Station St
Ingles St
Crockford St
PORT MELBOURNE
Farrell St
Albert St
Ross St
Graham St
Clark St

3

BEACON COVE
Swallow St
Princes St
Stokes St
Graham St
Princes St
Bridge St
Pool St
Bay St
Lyons St
Spring St
Glover St
Cruikshank St
Pickles St
Edwards Park
Lyell St
Mountain St
Tribe St
Iffla St
Glover St
Smith St
Beach St
Llardet St
St Vincent St
Greig St

4

Station Pier
Beach St
Nott St
Rouse St
Dow St
Esplanade W
Esplanade East
Johnston St
Graham St
Pickles St
Lagoon Reserve
Gasworks Arts Park
3
Bridport St W
Barrett St
Foote St
Danks St
Graham St
Reed St
Beaconsfield Pde

Station Pier
Spirit of Tasmania
4

5

Hobsons Bay

Ferries to Tasmania

N
0 _____ 500 m
0 _____ 0.25 miles

West Gate Fwy

City Rd

Kings Way

Chessell St
Market St
Ross St
York St
Coventry St
Dorcas St
Bank St

Moray St

South Melbourne Market

York St

Ferrars St

Cecil St

Clarendon St

SOUTH MELBOURNE

Sturt St

Eastern Rd

Tope St

Park St

Kings Way

Stead St

Albert Rd

St Kilda Rd

Dorcas St

Bank St

Montague St

Park St

Draper St

St Vincents Pl N
Anzac Gardens
St Vincent Gardens
St Vincents Pl S
Bevan St

Cardigan Pl

Brooke St

Victoria Ave

O'Grady St

Richardson St

ALBERT PARK

Phillipson St

Kerferd Rd

Cecil St

Martin St

Ferrars St

Dundas Pl

Montague St

Finlay St

Merton St

Kerferd Rd

Bridport St

Church St

Dow St
Napier St
Cobden St
Raglan St
Thomson St

Albert Rd

Albert Rd Dr

Melbourne Sports & Aquatic Centre

Albert Park

Herbert St

Carter St
Hambleton St
Erskine St
Richardson St
Harold St

Mills St

Page St
Little Page St
Danks St

MIDDLE PARK

Albert Park Lake

Gunn Island

Lakeside Dr

Albert Park Public Golf Course

Albert Park Lake

Canterbury Rd

Aughtie Dr

Lakeside Dr

Sights

Albert Park Lake
LAKE

1 Map p60, H4

Elegant black swans give their inimitable bottoms-up salute as you jog, cycle or walk the 5km perimeter of this constructed lake. Lakeside Dr was used as an international motor-racing circuit in the 1950s, and since 1996 the revamped track has been the venue for the Australian Formula One Grand Prix. Also on the periphery is the **Melbourne Sports & Aquatic Centre**, with an Olympic-size pool and child-delighting wave machine. (btwn Queens Rd, Fitzroy St, Aughtie Dr & Albert Rd, Albert Park; 🚊96)

South Melbourne Market
MARKET

2 Map p60, E2

The market's labyrinthine interior is packed to overflowing with an eccentric collection of stalls ranging from old-school to boutique. It's been on this site since 1864 and is a neighbourhood institution, as are its famous dim sims (sold here since 1949). There are plenty of atmospheric eateries and a lively night market on Thursdays from November to mid-December. There's a cooking school here, too – see the website for details. (www.southmelbournemarket.com.au; cnr Coventry & Cecil Sts, South Melbourne; ⏲8am-4pm Wed, Sat & Sun, to 5pm Fri; 🚊96)

Gasworks Arts Park
CULTURAL BUILDING

3 Map p60, D4

A taste of gritty Berlin in Melbourne, this former gas plant lay derelict from the 1950s before being developed into an arts precinct with red-brick galleries, a **theatre company** (check website for shows) and an ultra dog-friendly parkland. You can meet the artists on a guided tour or come for its summer **open-air cinema** or a **farmers market** (third Saturday of each month). (📞03-8606 4200; www.gasworks.org.au; cnr Graham & Pickles St, Albert Park; tours $25; ⏲tours 10.30am & 2pm Mon-Thu; 🚊1, 109)

Station Pier
LANDMARK

4 Map p60, A4

Melbourne's main sea passenger terminal, Station Pier has great sentimental associations for many migrants who arrived by ship in the 1950s and '60s, and for servicemen who used it during WWII. It has been

---

Understand
Formula One Grand Prix

These are the kind of figures that make petrolheads swoon: 300km/h, 950bhp and 19,000rpm. The 5.3km street circuit around normally tranquil Albert Park Lake is known for its smooth, fast surface. The buzz, both on the streets and in your ears, takes over Melbourne for four fully sick days in March.

South Melbourne Market

in operation since 1854, when the first major railway in Australia ran from here to the city. It's where the *Spirit of Tasmania,* cruise ships and navy vessels dock. (www.portofmelbourne.com; Waterfront Pl, Port Melbourne; 🚌109)

Eating

Albert Park Hotel
Oyster Bar & Grill SEAFOOD, PUB $$

 5 Map p60, E4

With a focus on oysters and seafood as well as bar food, this incarnation of the Albert Park Hotel (thanks again to Six Degrees) is filling seats with its promise of market-priced fish and wood-barbecued 'big fish' served in five different Mediterranean styles. (www.thealbertpark.com.au; cnr Montague St & Dundas Pl, Albert Park; mains $15-30; 🚌1, 96)

St Ali CAFE $$

 6 Map p60, F1

A hideaway warehouse conversion where the coffee is carefully sourced and guaranteed to be good. If you can't decide between house blend, specialty, black or white, there's a tasting 'plate' ($18). Awarded best food cafe in *The Age Good Cafe Guide 2013;* the corn fritters with poached eggs and haloumi are legendary. Off Clarendon St, between Coventry and York Sts. (☎03-9689 2990; www.stali.com.au; 12-18

Yarra Pl, South Melbourne; dishes $10-28; ⏱7am-6pm; 🚋112)

Mart 130

CAFE $$

7 Map p60, G5

A quirky location within the Federation-style Middle Park tram station, Mart 130 is a cute, sun-filled cafe that serves up corn fritters, toasted pide and big salads. Its deck overlooks the park with city views in the background. Weekend waits can be long. (📞03-9690 8831; 107 Canterbury Rd, Middle Park; mains $12-20; ⏱7.30am-4pm; 📶; 🚋96)

Jock's Ice-Cream

ICE CREAM $

8 Map p60, E4

For over a decade Jock has been scooping up his sorbets and ice creams made on site (baked apple, Baci, roast almond) to baysiders. Take-home tubs also available. (83 Victoria

---

Ave, Albert Park; single cones $4; ⏱noon-8pm Mon-Fri, to 10.30pm Sat & Sun; 🚋1)

Misuzu's

JAPANESE $$

9 Map p60, E4

Misuzu's menu includes whopping noodle, rice and curry dishes, tempuras and takeaway options from the neatly displayed sushi bar. Sit outside under lantern-hung trees, or inside surrounded by murals and dark wood. (📞03-9699 9022; 3-7 Victoria Ave, Albert Park; mains $18-30; ⏱lunch & dinner; 🚋1)

Drinking

Clement

CAFE

10 Map p60, F2

There's a buzz about this tiny cafe on the perimeter of the South Melbourne Market, not only for its expertly crafted brew but also for the homemade salted caramel or jam and custard doughnuts. Grab a streetside stool or takeaway and wander the market. (South Melbourne Market, 116-136 Cecil St, South Melbourne; ⏱7am-5pm; 🚋96)

Padre Coffee

CAFE

11 Map p60, E2

Offers a perfect (and popular) caffeine-enhanced respite from mad market shopping. (www.padrecoffee.com.au; Shop 33, South Melbourne Market; ⏱7am-4pm Wed, Sat & Sun, 7am-5pm Fri; 🚋96)

Local Life

Andrew's Burgers

A family-run burger institution, **Andrew's** (Map p60, E3; 📞03-9690 2126; www.andrewshamburgers.com.au; 144 Bridport St, Albert Park; burgers from $7.50; ⏱11am-3pm & 4.30-9pm Mon-Sat; 🚋1) has been around since the '50s. Its walls are still wood-panelled and are now covered with photos of local celebs who, like many, drop in for a classic burger with the lot and a big bag of chips to takeaway. Veg option available.

Top Tip

Market Discounts

For good deals on fresh produce, head to the South Melbourne Market (p62) near closing time, particularly on Sundays.

Matilda Bay Brewery

BREWERY

12 🚊 Map p60, B1

This microbrewery brews a great selection of beers on site, which you can sample right among its production equipment. Free tours on Saturdays. (📞03-9673 4545; www.matildabay.com.au; 89 Bertie St, Port Melbourne; 🕐11.30am-10pm Tue-Thu, to 11pm Fri & Sat; 🚊109)

Eve

CLUB

13 🚊 Map p60, F1

Florence Broadhurst wallpapers, a black granite bar and Louis chairs set the tone, which gets rapidly lower as the night progresses. Footballers, glamour girls and the odd lost soul come for cocktails and commercial house. Expect to queue after 9pm. Spencer St becomes Clarendon; it's near the corner of City Rd. (📞03-9696 7388; www.evebar.com.au; 334 City Rd, South Melbourne; 🕐dusk-late Thu-Sat; 🚊112)

Shopping

Avenue Books

BOOKS

14 🔒 Map p60, E4

Everyone needs a neighbourhood bookshop like this one. It's full of nooks and crannies to perch with literary fiction, cooking, gardening, art and children's books. Cluey staff make spot-on recommendations, too. (📞03-9690 2227; www.avenuebookstore.com.au; 127 Dundas Pl, Albert Park; 🕐9am-7pm; 🚊1)

Nest

HOMEWARES

15 🔒 Map p60, F2

This light, bright homewares store stocks SpaceCraft screen-printed textiles as well as Aesop skincare. It does its own range of cotton-knit 'comfort wear' that's way too nice to hide at home in. Staff are delightful. From South Melbourne Market head along Coventry St. (📞03-9699 8277; www.nesthomewares.com.au; 289 Coventry St, South Melbourne; 🚊96, 112)

South Yarra, Prahran & Windsor

These leafy well-to-do neighbourhoods have always been synonymous with glitz and glamour. Chapel St's South Yarra strip still parades itself as a must-do fashion destination, but these days it's about chain stores, tacky bars and, come sunset, doof-doof cars. Prahran and Windsor remain gutsy places, with designer stores, vintage clothing, lively bars and some refreshingly eclectic businesses.

The Sights in a Day

☀ Start with breakfast at the Observatory Cafe at the **Royal Botanic Gardens** (p68) or pack a picnic brunch. Stroll the grounds, feed the ducks and make your way through the park to pay your respects at the **Shrine of Remembrance** (p72), a monumental building dedicated to Australians at war.

☀ Then its time to venture into Prahran, starting at **Prahran Market** (p74) to browse fresh produce and gourmet food, and maybe sign up for a cooking class. Grab a top-notch coffee at **Market Lane** (p76), before hitting Chapel St for some serious shopping: for brand names and high-end boutiques go to the South Yarra end, for vintage and secondhand clothes head towards Windsor.

☾ There's plenty going on at night, with a huge choice of quality restaurants and nightlife at your fingers. Choose creative Thai dishes at funky **Colonel Tans** (p74), or go upmarket at **WoodLand House** (p74; formerly Jacques Reymond) – if you've booked well in advance. Fans of vodka won't want to miss **Borsch, Vodka & Tears** (p75) or cocktails at **Kid Boston** (p76), before kicking on to the dance floor at **Revolver Upstairs** (p76), one of Melbourne's best-loved night spots.

👁 Top Sights
Royal Botanic Gardens (p68)

♥ Best of Melbourne

Eating
WoodLand House (p74)

Colonel Tans (p74)

Drinking
Yellow Bird (p75)

Market Lane (p76)

Getting There

🚋 **Tram** 1, 3, 5, 6, 8, 16, 64, 67, 72, 78

🚆 **Train** South Yarra, Windsor

Top Sights
Royal Botanic Gardens

One of the finest botanical gardens in the world, the Royal Botanic Gardens is among Melbourne's most glorious attractions. Sprawling beside the Yarra River, the beautifully designed gardens feature a global selection of plantings and native Australian flora. Mini-ecosystems, such as a cacti and succulents area, a herb garden and an indigenous rainforest, are set amid vast lawns. Take a book, picnic or Frisbee – but most importantly, take your time.

◉ Map p70, A1

www.rbg.vic.gov.au

Birdwood Ave, South Yarra

admission free

⊙ 7.30am-sunset

🚍 Tourist Shuttle, 🚃 1, 3, 5, 6, 8, 16, 64, 67, 72

Don't Miss

Plant Collections

The gardens are home to thousands of plant species from around the globe. Some highlights include Fern Gully, which displays species typical of cool forests of Australasia. It's a particularly lovely place to stroll on a hot day, walking on winding paths along a stream and under the canopy of lush ferns. The camellia collection has around 800 different camellias and is at its best in winter; some of the plants date back to 1875.

Observatory

Stargazers won't want to miss the Melbourne Observatory, constructed from 1861 to 1863. Visitors can take a tour of the buildings with experienced guides from the Astronomical Society of Victoria and gaze up at the southern sky though historic telescopes.

Ian Potter Foundation Children's Garden

Kids will love the excellent, nature-based **Ian Potter Foundation Children's Garden** (⊘10am-4pm Wed-Sun, daily during Victorian school holidays, closed mid-Jul–mid-Sep), a whimsical and child-scaled place that invites kids and their parents to explore, discover and imagine.

Aboriginal Heritage Walk

The Royal Botanic Gardens are on a traditional camping and meeting place of the original Indigenous owners, and this **tour** (adult/child $25/10; ⊘11am Tue-Fri & 1st Sun of the month) takes you through their story – from songlines to plant lore, all in 90 fascinating minutes. The tour departs from the visitor centre.

☑ Top Tips

▶ A range of guided tours depart from the visitor centre, which is located at the former centre for stargazers. Choose from a variety of guided walks through assorted horticultural pockets to learn a bit about history, botany and wildlife.

▶ The gardens play host to the Moonlight Cinema (p78) and theatre performances during summer; check the website to see what's on.

▶ Pack a picnic blanket, a hat and sunscreen in case the shaded areas are taken.

✕ Take a Break

The best option, of course, is to pack your own picnic and grab a spot on the lawn. Otherwise, the **Observatory Cafe** at the main entrance is a good option for coffee, ice cream or a light lunch.

A
B
C
D
E
1
2
3
4
0
0
400 m
0.25 miles
RICHMOND
CREMORNE
SOUTH YARRA
Royal Botanic Gardens
Ornamental Lake
Herring Island
Herring Island Park
Como Park
Como House
Melbourne High School
Fawkner Park
Yarra River
CityLink (Monash Fwy)
M1
South Yarra
Aesop Spa
Alexandra Ave
Birdwood Ave
Domain Rd
Toorak Rd
Punt Rd
Williams Rd
Lechlade Ave
Como Ave
Kensington Rd
Hawksburn Rd
Rockley Rd
Tivoli Rd
River St
Malcolm St
Chapel St
Clara St
Oxford St
Palermo St
Chambers St
Claremont St
Yarra St
Darling St
Murphy St
Avoca St
Caroline St
Davis St
Powell St
Myrtle St
Macfarlan St
Caroline St S
Alexandra St
Lang St
Fawkner St
Ralston St
William St
Arthur St
Marne St
Leopold St
Park St
Millswyn St
Mary St
Brighton St
Balmain St
Church St
Chestnut St
Green St
Cubitt St
Dover St
Kelso St
Cremorne St
Walsh St
Clowes St
Anderson St
1
2
3
4
5
9
16
18
19

For reviews see

◉ Top Sights	p68
◉ Sights	p72
✖ Eating	p74
🍷 Drinking	p75
✖✖ Entertainment	p78
🛍 Shopping	p78

Sights

Shrine of Remembrance
MONUMENT

1 Map p70, A2

Beside St Kilda Rd stands the massive Shrine of Remembrance, built as a memorial to Victorians killed in WWI. It was built between 1928 and 1934, much of it with depression-relief, or 'susso', labour. Its bombastic classical design is partly based on the Mausoleum of Halicarnassus, one of the seven ancient wonders of the world. It's visible from the other end of town, and planning regulations continue

Local Life
The Tan
'Doing the Tan' is a ritual well-loved by Melburnians, and surprisingly it has nothing to do with the inside of a licensed premises. This 3.8km-long running **track** (Map p70, A1; Royal Botanic Gardens, Birdwood Ave, South Yarra; 🚌Tourist Shuttle, 🚃8), which takes in the outside perimeter of South Yarra's Royal Botanic Gardens, was once for well-shod horses, and is now one of Melbourne's most scenic places to sweat it out. Athletes and AFL footy stars often test their mettle here, but it is also well frequented by those happy to just shuffle or stroll its length. The current lap record was set by Australian Olympian runner Craig Mottram in 2006 at 10 minutes and 8 seconds.

to restrict any building that would obstruct the view of the shrine from Swanston St as far back as Lonsdale St. (www.shrine.org.au; Birdwood Ave, South Yarra; admission free; ⏰10am-5pm; 🚌Tourist Shuttle, 🚃1, 3, 5, 6, 8, 16, 64, 67, 72)

Como House
HISTORIC BUILDING

2 Map p70, E3

This grand colonial residence overlooking the Yarra was begun in 1840, and since faithfully restored by the National Trust. It contains some of the belongings of the Armytage family, the last and longest owners, who lived in the house for 95 years. Opening hours are irregular, usually a few showings per month (call ahead for times and bookings), which will allow you to stroll its extensive, well-tended grounds, which are faithful to 19th-century landscaping principles and include a croquet lawn and magnificent flower walks. (📞03-9827 2500, tour bookings 03-8663 7260; www.comohouse. com.au; cnr Williams Rd & Lechlade Ave, South Yarra; adult/child/family $15/9/35; ⏰10am-4pm; 🚃8)

Government House
HISTORIC BUILDING

3 Map p70, A2

On the outer edge of the Botanic Gardens, the Italianate-style Government House was built in 1872 and has been the residence of all serving Victorian governors since. A replica of Queen Victoria's palace on England's Isle of Wight, as well as being the royal pied-

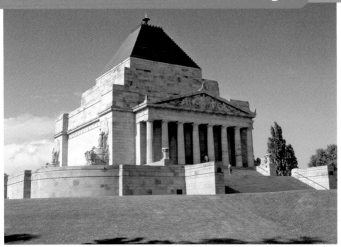

Shrine of Remembrance

à-terre, the house and gardens are also used for an array of state functions and celebrations. Book well in advance to take the National Trust's two-hour tour on Monday and Thursday. (☎03-9656 9804; www.nationaltrust.org.au; Kings Domain, South Yarra; tours adult/child $18/10; ◻Tourist Shuttle, ◻1, 3, 5, 6, 8, 16, 64, 67, 72)

Herring Island Park   PARK

4 ◉ Map p70, E2

Herring Island is a prelapsarian garden that seeks to preserve the original trees and grasses of the Yarra and provide a home for indigenous animals. Within is an impressive collection of environmental sculpture, including work by Andy Goldsworthy (UK) and locals Julie Collins, Robert Jacks and Robert Bridgewater. There are designated picnic and BBQ areas. On weekends during summer, a Parks Victoria punt operates from Como Landing on Alexandra Ave in South Yarra; other times you'll need a kayak to get here. (www.parkweb.vic.gov.au; Alexander Ave, South Yarra; ◻8, 78, ◻Burnley)

Aesop Spa   DAY SPA

5 ◉ Map p70, C3

Aesop Spa takes it up a notch – you can choose from five basic treatments, and your lactate surge or detox overhaul will be further customised to your skin while you're wrapped up in a mohair blanket on a cotton futon. (☎03-9866

5250; www.aesop.com/au; 153 Toorak Rd, South Yarra; treatments from $120; ⊗by appointment 10am-4pm Wed-Sat; 🚊8, 🚉South Yarra)

Eating

WoodLand House
MODERN AUSTRALIAN **$$$**

6 Map p70, E7

Housed in a Victorian terrace of ample proportions, this was the former incarnation of Jacques Reymond, a local pioneer of degustation dining. After 15 years he handed over the reins to two of his sous chefs, who learned everything they know from the man.

The tasting menu has shifted from its original French focus to an innovative Modern Australian direction incorporating quality local produce. Sunday lunch offers a good-value chef's set menu of four courses for $80. (📞03-9525 2178; www.woodlandhouse. com.au; 78 Williams Rd, Prahran; tasting menu from $115; ⊗noon-3pm Thu, Fri & Sun, 6.30-9pm Tue-Sat; 🚉6)

Colonel Tans
THAI **$$**

Set up in the back corner of Revolver Upstairs (see 13 Map p70, C6), funky Colonel Tans is run by the same team who do the city centre's Cookie (p38), with similarly yummy creative Thai fusion dishes from traditional curries and tangy snapper rolled in betel leaf to kaffir-lime chicken burgers. (📞03-9521 5985; www.coloneltans.com.au; 229 Chapel St, Prahran; dishes $15; ⊗5-11pm Tue-Sat, from noon Fri; 🚉6, 🚉Prahran)

Valentino
ITALIAN **$$**

7 Map p70, E6

Offering Calabrian-style dishes with a lively welcoming atmosphere, Valentino has a wonderful antipasti selection – but its pizzas are the real reason to come here. Great *apertivi* and wine list, too. (📞03-9826 8815; www.valentinorestaurant.com.au; 517 Malvern Rd, Hawksburn; pizzas $20; ⊗noon-2pm Fri-Sun, 5.30-10pm Tue-Sun; 🚉72)

Dino's
SPANISH **$$**

8 Map p70, C8

The wine list's longer than the food list (evidence of prior drinking

---

Local Life
Prahran Market

The **Prahran Market** (Map p70, C5; www.prahranmarket.com.au; 163 Commercial Rd, Prahran; ⊗7am-5pm Tue, Thu & Sat, to 7pm Fri, 10am-3pm Sun; 🚊72, 78, 🚉Prahran) has been an institution for over a century. It's one of the finest produce markets in the city, with numerous stalls stocking fresh seafood, deli items, fruits and vegetables. The market is also home to a culinary store, **Essential Ingredient** (📞03-9827 9047; www.essentialingredient. com.au; classes $110-275); check the website for details of its cooking school, which features workshops with Melbourne's most lauded chefs.

lines the walls), but it's a great spot to dine on ex-Cumulus Inc chef's breakfast *bocadillos* (sandwiches) in the early hours and Spanish tapas flavours after dark. Opposite Windsor Station, it can get very busy. (📞03-9521 3466; 34 Chapel St, Windsor; mains $20-32; ⏰8am-midnight; 🚊5, 64, 78, 79, 🚉Windsor)

Da Noi
ITALIAN $$

 9 Map p70, B3

Da Noi serves up beautiful Sardinian dishes that change daily. The spontaneous kitchen might reinterpret the chef's special three times a night. Just go with it; it's a unique experience and harks back to a different way of dining. Bookings advised. (📞03-9866 5975; 95 Toorak Rd, South Yarra; mains $35, 4-course tasting menu $93; ⏰noon-3pm & 6-10pm Mon-Sat; 🚊8, 🚉South Yarra)

Drinking

Yellow Bird
BAR

 10 Map p70, C7

Keeps Windsor's cool kids happy with all-day drinks (including an evil coffee, sugar and beer shot) and diner-style food. Owned by the drummer from Something for Kate, its rock 'n' roll ambience is genuine, with a passing cast of musos and a fantastic playlist of underground bands. (📞03-9533 8983; www.yellowbird.com.au; 122

JAMES BRAUND / GETTY IMAGES ©

Da Noi

Chapel St, Windsor; ⏰7.30am-late; 🚊78, 79, 🚉Windsor)

Borsch, Vodka & Tears
BAR

 11 Map p70, C7

This place is *the* business for sampling vodka. The extensive list covers a range of clear, oak-matured, fruit-infused and traditional *nalewka kresowa* (made according to old Russian and Polish recipes); knowledgeable staff can help you choose your shot. Line your stomach with some excellent borsch or blintzes. There's another one in Elsternwick with 140 types of vodka and contemporary Eastern European dishes. (www.borschvodkaandtears.com; 173 Chapel St, Windsor; 🚊6, 🚉Prahran)

Dukes   CAFE

12 🚇 Map p70, C7

Exposed brick and wood beams give this Windsor cafe a warm feel and the perfect ambience for downing one of its coffees, expertly made from beans roasted on site. (www.dukescoffee.com.au; 169 Chapel St, Windsor; ⏱7am-4pm Mon-Sat, 8am-4pm Sun; 🚊6, 78, 79)

Revolver Upstairs   CLUB

13 🚇 Map p70, C6

Rowdy Revolver can feel like an enormous version of your lounge room, but with 54 hours of nonstop music come the weekend, you're probably glad it's not. Live music, interesting DJs and film screenings keep the mixed crowd wide awake. (www.revolverupstairs.com.au; 229 Chapel St, Prahran; ⏱noon-4am Tue-Fri, 24hr Sat & Sun; 🚊6, 🚈Prahran)

🔍 Local Life
Windsor Castle Hotel

This backstreet art deco building is full of cosy nooks, sunken pits, fireplaces and flocked wallpaper – all of which make the **Windsor Castle** (Map p70, B8; 89 Albert St, Windsor; ⏱3pm-late Mon-Thu, noon-late Fri & Sun; 🚊5, 64, 🚈Windsor) extremely attractive...but it's the tiki-themed beer garden that makes it great.

Market Lane   CAFE

14 🚇 Map p70, C5

Market Lane is the perfect pick-me-up after poring over gourmet goodies at the Prahran Market. All roasting is done on site, producing some of the best brew in the city. Come Friday and Saturdays for the free cuppings (tastings) from 10am to 11am. (www.marketlane.com.au; Prahran Market, 163 Commercial Rd, Prahran; ⏱7am-5pm Tue-Sat, 8am-5pm Sun; 🚊72, 78, 79)

Kid Boston   BAR

15 🚇 Map p70, C8

The best cocktails this side of the river. This tiny Windsor newbie has arrived in style, with top-shelf martinis, high ballers, sours and aperitifs to go with a delicious menu of bar food. (www.kidboston.com.au; 44 Chapel St, Windsor; ⏱5pm-late Mon-Fri, 3pm-late Sat & Sun; 🚊78, 79, 🚈Windsor)

Drugstore Espresso   CAFE

16 🚇 Map p70, C4

Just the place to re-energise from a bout of Chapel St shopping fatigue, with twice-weekly-changing single-origin coffees and a selection of hearty-sized sandwiches and wagyu beef burgers. (www.drugstoreespresso.com.au; 194 Toorak Rd, South Yarra; ⏱7am-4pm Mon-Fri, 8am-4pm Sat & Sun; 🛜; 🚊8, 🚈South Yarra)

Understand
Cafes & Coffee Culture

Cafes are an integral part of Melbourne life. Many city-dwellers are up early to catch up with colleagues or to read the newspaper over a latte and a slice of sourdough before the workday begins. Weekends see cafes across the city fill (queues are not uncommon) with those looking for a long blow-out breakfast.

While socialising is a big part of this ritual, the coffee itself is in no way an afterthought. Melbourne's coffee is far superior to what you'll get in London or Los Angeles, and often tops what you'll find in Italy. Neighbourhood cafes have begun to attract the kind of tribal devotion reserved for AFL teams. Flavoured coffee? Forget about it. Yes, big chains such as Starbucks have sprung up, but an attempt to settle in Lygon St didn't last long – why would you need a cookie-cutter multinational to tell you how it's done when Melbourne's been getting the crema correct for well over 20 years?

The cafe tradition goes back to the early years of last century, with the arrival of Victoria's first wave of Italian and Greek migrants, but really took off post-WWII when large numbers of Italians settled in the inner city and the first Gaggia and La Cimbali espresso machines were imported under licence in 1953. Bourke St's Pellegrini's is an ever-enchanting survivor of this generation. The brew may be unremarkable by today's standards, but the Italian brio, urban bonhomie and original decor are as authentic as it gets. Melbourne *torrefazione* (Italian coffee roasters) such as Genovese and Grinders also date back to this era, and their bean blends now fuel cafes all over the country. Other local roasters include Atomic, Jasper and Gravity, and Castlemaine's Coffee Basics.

While these original family-run roasters have prospered and become household names, Melbourne is now firmly in the grip of coffee's third wave. Coffee talk now runs to terroir, and single-origin beans, premium small-batch roasts and alternative brewing methods such as siphon, pour-over, filter and cold-drip have taken coffee appreciation to a new level. Melbourne is in an era of extreme coffee excellence.

Onesixone

CLUB

17 Map p70, C7

Front up to the peephole – if you pass muster, snaffle a couch or a pouffe. A wiggle on the small dance floor is obligatory. Late-night Saturdays start at 4am and run until the rest of the world is truly up and about. (☎03-9533 8433; www.onesixone.com.au; 161 High St, Prahran; ☻hours vary Thu-Sat; ☒6, ☒Prahran)

Entertainment

Sidney Myer Music Bowl

CONCERT VENUE

18 Map p70, A1

This beautiful amphitheatre in the park is used for a variety of outdoor events, from the **Tropfest** film festival to Nick Cave and the Bad Seeds, Opera in the Bowl or the New Year's Day rave **Summerdayze**. (☎1300 182 183; www.artscentremelbourne.com.au; Linlithgow Ave, Kings Domain Gardens; ☒1, 3, 5, 6, 8, 16, 64, 67, 72)

Top Tip

Vintage Clothing
If you're keen to hunt out second-hand clothing, head down to the Windsor end of Chapel St, where you'll find a mix of op shops, vintage clothing stores and boutiques that have a top range of original and cheap clothes.

Moonlight Cinema

CINEMA

19 Map p70, A1

Melbourne's original outdoor cinema, with the option of 'Gold Grass' tickets that include a glass of wine and a reserved bean-bag bed. (www.moonlight. com.au; Gate D, Royal Botanic Gardens, Birdwood Ave, South Yarra; ☒8)

Red Stitch Actors Theatre

THEATRE

20 Map p70, C8

This independent company stages new international works that are often premieres in Australia. The tiny black-box theatre, opposite the Astor and down the end of the driveway, is a cosy space. (☎03-9533 8082; www.redstitch.net; Rear, 2 Chapel St, Windsor; ☒5, 64, 78, 79, ☒Windsor)

Astor

CINEMA

21 Map p70, C8

See a double feature for the price of one. Screens a mix of recent releases, art-house films and classics in art deco surrounds. (☎03-9510 1414; www.astortheatre.net.au; cnr Chapel St & Dandenong Rd, Windsor; ☒5, 64, 78, ☒Windsor)

Shopping

Chapel Street Bazaar

VINTAGE

22 Map p70, C6

Calling this a 'permanent undercover collection of market stalls' won't give you any clue to what's tucked away here. This old arcade is a retro-obsessive riot. It doesn't matter if Italian art glass, vintage furniture or Noddy egg cups are your thing, you'll find it here. There's a mix of cluttered mayhem and well-organised boutiquey stalls. (☎03-9521 3174; 217-223 Chapel St, Prahran; ☺10am-6pm; 🚌78, 79, 🚉Prahran)

Fat FASHION, ACCESSORIES

23 🔒 Map p70, C6

The Fat empire has changed the way Melbourne dresses, catapulting a fresh generation of designers into the city's consciousness, including Claude Maus, Dr Denim, Kloke and Status Anxiety. There's another branch in Fitzroy. (www.fat4.com; 272 Chapel St, Prahran; ☺10am-6pm Mon-Sat, 11am-5pm Sun; 🚌78, 79, 🚉Prahran)

Shelley Panton HOMEWARES, GIFTS

24 🔒 Map p70, E6

Potter Shelley Panton has recently set up this beautiful store, stocking her own local wares alongside other local designers' work and imported goodies from around the world. Pick up some ecofriendly bamboo dinnerware, copper pendant lighting or Indian loom rugs. (www.shelleypanton.com; 440 Malvern Rd, Prahran; ☺9am-7pm Mon-Wed & Fri, to 9pm Thu, 10am-5.30pm Sat & Sun; 🚌72)

Greville Records

Greville Records MUSIC

25 🔒 Map p70, C6

One of the last bastions of the 'old' Greville St, this fabulous music shop has such a loyal following that the great Neil Young invited the owners on stage during a Melbourne concert. It's now very much geared towards vinyl. (www.grevillerecords.com.au; 152 Greville St, Prahran; ☺10am-6pm Mon-Sat, to 7pm Fri, noon-5pm Sun; 🚌78, 79)

VINEGAR

Explore

East Melbourne & Richmond

Once a ragtag collection of workers' cottages inhabited by generations of labourers, Richmond is a genteel suburb home to the Melbourne Cricket Ground, excellent pubs and a thriving Vietnamese community along Victoria St. Across Punt Rd leading into the city, East Melbourne boasts sedate, wide streets lined with grand double-fronted Victorian terraces, Italianate mansions and art deco apartments.

The Sights in a Day

Start the day along Bridge Rd with breakfast and good coffee at **Touchwood** (p87). Wander up the road afterwards to shop for some discount big-name brands. Explore Richmond's character-filled backstreets to link up with Swan St for more shopping and cafes, and a carnivorous lunch at **Meatmother** (p86).

If you're visiting on the weekend, you may be lucky enough to catch a game of footy or cricket at the **Melbourne Cricket Ground** (p82), otherwise you can visit its hallowed turf on a tour at the **National Sports Museum** (p83) on-site. Across the bridge, sporting buffs can continue their day with a tour of **Melbourne Park** (p89), home to the Australian Tennis Open, or even rent a practice court for a hit. Next up, **AAMI Park** (p89), where Melbourne's rugby and soccer teams battle it out.

Head to Richmond's Victoria St for dinner at one of its many Vietnamese restaurants for inexpensive Southeast Asian dishes. Most, including **Minh Minh** (p86), allow you to bring your own (BYO) alcohol, making it a social occasion. Afterwards, catch a gig at the **Corner Hotel** (p87) or grab a beer upstairs at its buzzing rooftop bar.

 Top Sights

Melbourne Cricket Ground (p82)

 Best of Melbourne

Entertainment

Melbourne Cricket Ground (p82)

Corner Hotel (p87)

Eating

Demitri's Feast (p85)

Minh Minh (p86)

Getting There

🚋 **Tram** 48, 70, 75, 78

🚆 **Train** Richmond, East Richmond

Top Sights
Melbourne Cricket Ground

In a city that prides itself as the sporting capital of Australia, the Melbourne Cricket Ground (MCG) takes centre stage. With a capacity of 100,000 people, the 'G' is one of the world's great sporting venues, hosting cricket in the summer and AFL footy in the winter, and for many Australians it's considered hallowed ground. Make it to a game if you can (highly recommended), but otherwise you can still make your pilgrimage on non-match days for its National Sports Museum and ground tour.

◉ Map p84, B3

☎03-9657 8888

www.mcg.org.au

tours adult/child/family $20/10/50

⏰tours 10am-3pm

🚌Tourist Shuttle, 🚊48, 70, 75, 🚉Jolimont

Don't Miss

AFL Footy Games

Attending a game of AFL footy at a packed MCG is a memorable experience among the atmosphere of 80,000 parochial fans. The game is known for its cracking pace, aerial grabs, long-shot goals, intense physicality and athleticism. The season runs from mid-March to the end of September; tickets are mostly available on match days.

Cricket Matches

Cricket is Victoria's summer love and seeing a test at the 'G' is a must for cricket fans from around the world. The Boxing Day Test is for many sport-mad Melburnians a bigger deal than Christmas itself. Warm days, cricket's leisurely pace and the supporters who've travelled from far and wide often make for spectator theatrics.

National Sports Museum

Hidden beneath the MCG, the **National Sports Museum** (☏03-9657 8856; www.nsm.org.au; MCG, Olympic Stand, Gate 3 ; adult/concession/family $20/10/50, with MCG tour $30/15/60; ⏱10am-5pm)features five permanent exhibitions focusing on Australia's favourite sports and celebrates historic sporting moments. Kids will love the interactive section where they can test their skills. Items on display include handwritten notes used to define the rules of Australian Rules Football in 1859; a who's who of Aussie cricket's green caps (including Don Bradman's); AFL Brownlow medals; and Cathy Freeman's famous Sydney Olympics swift suit.

Ground Tours

On non-match days, go behind the scenes on tours through the stands, media and coaches' areas, into change rooms and out onto the ground.

☑ **Top Tips**

▶ There are no ground tours on game days.

▶ Discounts are available if you get a combined museum and tour ticket.

▶ If you're in the area and after a taste of a live AFL game, sometimes it's possible to wander in free of charge at three-quarter time (around 1½ hours after starting time) to see the last 30 minutes of the action.

✗ **Take a Break**

There's no shortage of pubs in the immediate area for a pre-game drink, with the rooftop bar at the Corner Hotel (p87) being a lively choice. Richmond Hill Cafe & Larder (p86), at the top of Bridge Rd, is a tasty spot for lunch or breakfast if you're doing a tour of the ground.

Sights

Fitzroy Gardens PARK

1 Map p84 , B1

The city drops away suddenly just east of Spring St, giving way to Melbourne's beautiful backyard, the Fitzroy Gardens. The stately avenues lined with English elms, flower beds, expansive lawns, strange fountains and a creek are a short stroll from town. The highlight is **Cooks' Cottage** (☎03-9419 5766; www.cookscottage. com.au; adult/child/family $5/2.50/13.50; ⊙9am-5pm), shipped brick by brick from Yorkshire and reconstructed in 1934 (the cottage actually belonged to the navigator's parents). It's decorated in mid-18th-century style, with an exhibition about Captain James Cook's eventful, if controversial, voyages to the Southern Ocean. (www.fitzroygardens.com; Wellington Pde, btwn Lansdowne & Albert Sts, East Melbourne; ☒ Tourist Shuttle, ☒ 75, ☒ Jolimont)

Cooks' Cottage, Fitzroy Gardens

GERRY WHITMONT / GETTY IMAGES ©

Johnston Collection MUSEUM

2 Map p84, B2

Making for a fascinating visit, not only will you see the exquisite collection of sharp-eyed antique dealer William Johnston in his majestic East Melbourne mansion, but you'll hear his intriguing back story. It's popular with repeat visitors as the furniture and items are changed every three months – different curators, usually an artist or designer, thematically rearrange the house from Johnston's collection. Tours depart from Hilton on the Park, leaving three times daily. Booking is required. (☎03-9416 2515; www.johnstoncollection.org; East Melbourne; adult/concession $25/23; ☒ 48, 75)

Eating

Demitri's Feast GREEK $

3 Map p84, D4

Don't even attempt to get a seat here on a weekend; aim for a quiet weekday, when you'll have time and space to fully immerse yourself in lunches such as calamari salad with ouzo aioli. (www. demitrisfeast.com.au; 141 Swan St, Richmond;

mains $14-16; ⏱7.30am-4.30pm Tue-Fri, from 8am Sat & Sun; 🚊70, 🚉East Richmond)

Meatmother
AMERICAN $$

4 🍴 Map p84, D4

Vegetarians beware: this eatery doubles as a shrine to the slaughterhouse, evident in the meat cleavers hanging on the walls and blood-dripping animal skeleton prints. All meat is smoked over oak, from the eight-hour smoked pork sandwich to the beef brisket. Messy up your chops with a dinner meat tray and a side of chipotle slaw and raise your glass of American whiskey to Meatmother. (www.meatmother.com.au; 167 Swan St, Richmond; lunch trays $14, dinner trays $19-23; ⏱6pm-late Tue, noon-3pm & 6pm-late Wed-Sun; 🚊70, 78, 79)

Minh Minh
VIETNAMESE, LAOTIAN $

5 🍴 Map p84, D1

Minh Minh specialises in fiery Laotian dishes – the herby green-and-red-chilli beef salad is a favourite – but does Vietnamese staples, too. (☎03-9427 7891;

Local Life
Old-School Vietnamese
Head upstairs to **Thy Thy 1** (Map p84, D1; ☎03-9429 1104; 1st fl, 142 Victoria St, Richmond; mains from $9; ⏱9am-10pm; 🚊109, 🚉North Richmond), a Victoria St original (unchanged since 1987), for cheap and delicious Vietnamese. No corkage for bring-your-own (BYO) booze.

94 Victoria St, Richmond; mains $10-18; ⏱4-10pm Tue, 11.30am-10.30pm Wed, Thu & Sun, to 11pm Fri & Sat; 🚊109, 🚉North Richmond)

Baby
PIZZA $$

6 🍴 Map p84, E4

Ignore the porno light feature and get into the food and vibe: delicious pizza, the occasional Aussie TV star and many, many trendy folk. It's busy, bold and run by restaurant king Christopher Lucas, so it's quite brilliant. Even for a pizza joint. (☎03-9421 4599; www.babypizza.com.au; 631-633 Church St; mains $17; ⏱7am-11pm; 🚊70, 78, 🚉East Richmond)

Richmond Hill Cafe & Larder
CAFE $$

7 🍴 Map p84, C3

Once the domain of well-known cook Stephanie Alexander, Richmond Hill still boasts its lovely cheese room and simple, comforting foods such as cheesy toast. There are breakfast cocktails for the brave. (☎03-9421 2808; www.rhcl.com.au; 48-50 Bridge Rd, Richmond; lunch $12-26; ⏱8.30am-4.30pm; 🚊75, 🚉West Richmond)

Drinking

Bar Economico
BAR

8 🍷 Map p84, D4

The newspapered front windows might have you turning on your heel, but rest assured you're in the right place. With its menus on ripped cardboard boxes and caged bar, Economico is a kind of Central American dive bar specialising in rum-based cocktails – Wrong Island Iced Tea sums the place up nicely. Buy your drink tickets from the booth first, then redeem them at the bar. (438 Church St, Richmond; ⏱5pm-late Wed-Sat, 2pm-late Sun; 🚊70, 79, 🚉East Richmond)

Touchwood   CAFE

9 Map p84, E3

A light, airy cafe with plenty of space, both indoors and out in the courtyard, serving single-origin coffee in a former recycled furniture store (hence: Touchwood). (www.touchwoodcafe.com; 480 Bridge Rd, Richmond; ⏱7am-4pm Mon-Fri, 7.30am-4.30pm Sat & Sun; 🚊48, 75)

Collection   BAR

10 Map p84, E3

Another bar Americana, this swampy New Orleans watering hole has big glass jars of gin and bourbon resting on its polished bar and a menu of Cajun-Creole cooking, including dishes with crocodile (no alligator, sorry), gumbo ya ya and crab sandwiches. (www.thecollectionbar.com.au; 328 Bridge Rd, Richmond; ⏱4pm-1am Tue-Sun; 🚊48, 75)

Public House   BAR

11 Map p84, E4

Not in any way resembling a public house from any period of history, this great Six Degrees fit-out features the signature blend of found glass and

 Local Life

Mountain Goat Brewery

In the backstreets of industrial Richmond, the local microbrewery **Mountain Goat** (www.goatbeer.com.au; cnr North & Clark Sts, Richmond; ⏱5pm-midnight Wed & Fri; 🚊48, 75, 109, 🚉Burnley) is set in a massive beer-producing warehouse, where you can enjoy its range of beers (including $11 tasting paddles) while nibbling on pizza. There are free brewery tours on Wednesdays. It's tricky to reach: head down Bridge Rd, turn left at Burnley St and right at North St.

earthy raw and recycled materials. There's imported beer on tap, jugs of Pimms and a short but sweet wine list. DJs set up on weekends and attract a young good-looking crowd ready to, uh, mingle. (☎03-9421 0187; www.publichouse.com.au; 433-435 Church St, Richmond; ⏱noon-late Tue-Sun; 🚊70, 79, 🚉East Richmond)

Entertainment

Corner Hotel   LIVE MUSIC

12 Map p84, D4

The band room here is one of Melbourne's most popular midsized venues and has seen plenty of loud and live action over the years, from Dinosaur Jr to the Buzzcocks. If your ears need a break, there's a friendly front bar. The rooftop has city views, but gets

Understand
Sporting Mad Melbourne

Cynics snicker that sport is the sum of Victoria's culture, although it's hard to hear them above all that cheering, theme-song singing and applause. Victorians do take the shared spectacle of the playing field very seriously. It's undeniably the state's most dominant expression of common beliefs and behaviour, and brings people from all backgrounds together.

Melbourne hosts a disproportionate number of international sporting events, including the Australian Open, Australian Formula One Grand Prix and Melbourne Cup horse race. The city's arenas, tracks, grounds and courts are regarded as the world's best developed and most well situated cluster of facilities. Victoria is home to more major events, such as the Rip Curl Pro (aka Bells Beach Surf Classic) and the Australian Motorcycle Grand Prix on Phillip Island.

At the heart of its obsession is Australian Rules Football (AFL, Aussie Rules or 'the footy'), born in Melbourne in 1858. Today it's followed fanatically, and games regularly attract crowds of 50,000 to 90,000 during the season that runs from March to September. During grand final week the whole city comes to grips with finals fever.

Cricket is Victoria's summer passion and it's the game that truly unites the state with the rest of Australia. It has a stronghold in Victoria, given the hallowed tuf of the Melbourne Cricket Ground (MCG) and Cricket Australia's base in Melbourne.

Between footy and cricket seasons, Melburnians choose horseracing as their obsession during the Spring Carnival in October. It culminates with 'the race that stops a nation': the Melbourne Cup, held on the first Tuesday of November. It attracts 120,000 spectators, and marks a public holiday.

The 'rectangle' football codes – rugby league (NRL), rugby union and soccer – are also well supported. In the A-League national soccer competition (October to May), Melbourne is represented by two teams, Melbourne Victory and Melbourne City, who both play at the striking honeycomb-roofed AAMI Park. Likewise Melbourne Storm in the National Rugby League (NRL) and the Melbourne Rebels in the Super Rugby (Super 15). International rugby union tests are held yearly in Melbourne at Docklands Stadium.

Understand
MCG Dreaming

Where did Australian Rules Football (AFL) come from? There's plenty of evidence to suggest that Aboriginal men and women played a form of football (called 'marngrook') prior to white settlement. Did they play it at the MCG site? The MCG has two scar trees from which bark was removed by Aboriginal people to make canoes. These reminders make it clear that Melbourne's footy fans (and perhaps players) were not the first to gather at the site of the MCG – or the Melbourne Corroboree Ground, as some Indigenous Australians like to call it.

superpacked, and often with a different crowd from the music fans below. (📞03-9427 9198; www.cornerhotel.com; 57 Swan St, Richmond; ⏰4pm-late Tue & Wed, noon-late Thu-Sun; 🚋70, 🚆Richmond)

Melbourne Park   TENNIS, BASKETBALL
13 ⭐ Map p84, A3

Home to the **Australian Open** tennis Grand Slam held in January, Melbourne Park precinct has 34 courts including its centerpiece **Rod Laver Arena**. You can take a tour to the dressing rooms, VIP areas and superboxes. Its indoor court hire ranges from $36 to $42, and outdoor courts cost between $28 and $36, plus racquet hire.

As well as tennis, **Hisense Arena** is also home to the Melbourne Tigers basketball team in the NBL (National Basketball League), and the Melbourne Vixens netball team. Nearby **Olympic Park** hosts athletics. (📞03-9286 1600; www.mopt.com.au; Batman Ave, Richmond; tours adult/child/family $15/7/35; 🚋48, 70, 75, 🚆Jolimont)

AAMI Park   SOCCER, RUGBY
14 ⭐ Map p84, B4

Across from Rod Laver Arena, AAMI Park is home to Melbourne's soccer and rugby teams. With a capacity of 30,000, its rectangular pitch is enclosed within a striking honeycombed-bioframe stadium. (📞03-9286 1600; www.aamipark. com.au; Olympic Blvd, Richmond; tickets from $30; 🚋70, 🚆Richmond)

Shopping

Lily & the Weasel   HOMEWARES, GIFTS
15 🔒 Map p84, D4

Lily & the Weasel stocks a mix of beautiful things from around the globe alongside stuff from local designers. Screenprints of iconic Richmond landmarks make for great souvenirs, as do wooden children's toys, Otto & Spike scarves and Robert Gordon ceramics. (www.lilyandtheweasel.com.au; 173 Swan St, Richmond; ⏰11am-6pm Tue-Fri, 10am-5pm Sat, 11am-4pm Sun; 🚋70, 78)

Local Life
East Brunswick

Getting There

Brunswick and East
Brunswick are easily
accessed 20 minutes
from the city.

🚋 1, 8, 19, 96

🚆 Brunswick

Multicultural Brunswick is a wonderful mix of
Middle Eastern, Greek, African and Indian immigrants, who converge on Sydney Rd to create a
lively strip with some fantastic eating. More recent
times have seen an influx of the younger hip crowd
who've added another layer of vibrancy, particularly in East Brunswick, which has some of Melbourne's coolest bars and cafes along Lygon St.

❶ Brunch at Pope Joan

Pope Joan (☏03-9388 8858; www.popejoan.com.au; 77-79 Nicholson St, East Brunswick; mains $15; ⏱7.30am-11pm Mon-Fri, until 5pm Sat & Sun; ☐96) has a menu of creative comfort food, strong coffee and 'liquid breakfasts' of Bloody Marys and spritzers.

❷ Sustainable Stopover

Ceres (☏03-9389 0100; www.ceres.org.au; 8 Lee St, East Brunswick; admission free; ⏱9am-5pm, market 9am-2pm Wed & Sat, to 5pm Thu & Fri; ☐96) is a two-decades-old community environment built on a former rubbish tip. Take a stroll around the permaculture and bush-food nursery, community market and the great bookstore.

❸ Get Caffeinated

A big player in Melbourne's coffee movement, warehouse-style cafe **Brunswick East Project** (☏03-9381 1881; www.padrecoffee.com.au; 483 Lygon St, East Brunswick; ⏱7am-4pm Mon-Sat, 8am-4pm Sun; ☐1, 8) is the original roaster for Padre Coffee and brews its own premium single-origins.

❹ Something Sweet

Mismatched cutlery and crockery makes **Sugardough** (www.sugardough.com.au; 163 Lygon St, East Brunswick; mains $8; ⏱7.30am-5pm Tue-Fri, to 4pm Sat & Sun; ☐1, 8) a bit like grandma's place on family reunion day. It does a roaring trade in pastries, pies (including vegetarian) and breads.

❺ Predinner Drink

East Brunswick's end of Lygon St has a stellar choice of watering holes. The **Alderman** (134 Lygon St, East Brunswick; ⏱5pm-late Tue-Fri, 2pm-late Sat & Sun; ☎; ☐1, 8) is your classic East Brunswick local: inviting wooden bar, open fireplace, good beer selection, cocktails by the jug and a courtyard.

❻ Dinner at Rumi

Rumi (☏03-9388 8255; www.rumirestaurant.com.au; 116 Lygon St, East Brunswick; mains $17-23; ⏱6-10pm; ☐1, 8) serves traditional Lebanese cooking and contemporary interpretations of old Persian dishes. The *sigara boregi* (cheese and pine-nut pastries) are a local institution, and tasty mains are balanced with an interesting selection of vegetable dishes.

❼ Craft Beer Time

The **Alehouse Project** (☏03-9387 1218; www.thealehouseproject.com.au; 98-100 Lygon St, East Brunswick; ⏱3pm-late Tue-Fri, noon-late Sat & Sun; ☎; ☐1, 8) is where beer lovers convene and compare notes on the 12 craft beers on tap. Beer-hall-style seating, op-shop couches and a courtyard.

❽ Live Music

The **Retreat** (☏03-9380 4090; www.retreathotelbrunswick.com.au; 280 Sydney Rd, Brunswick; ⏱noon-late; ☐19, ☒Brunswick) is a beloved Brunswick venue, a 15-minute walk or short cab ride away on Sydney Rd. Find your habitat – garden backyard, grungy band room or intimate front bar – and relax.

Explore

Fitzroy & Collingwood

Despite a long bout of gentrification, the grungy inner-north suburbs of Fitzroy and Collingwood still maintain their reputation as the place where the cool kids hang out. Today it's more about meeting to 'do' lunch and blog about it before checking out the offerings at local 'one-off' boutiques, cafes, bars and galleries along Smith and Gertrude Sts.

The Sights in a Day

☀ Start in the gritty backstreets of Collingwood, with an Ethiopian single-sourced coffee and 'avocado smash' at **Proud Mary** (p101). Then see where Melbourne's contemporary art scene is at in the **Collingwood Arts Precinct** (p98).

☀ Venture down Smith St for lunch, and choose from favs such as **Huxtaburger** (p99) for brioche-bun burgers or **Gelato Messina** (p98) for life-changing gelato. Take in Smith St's bearded and tattooed brigade, and head around the corner to Gertrude St for some of Melbourne's trendiest boutique stores including **Third Drawer Down** (p103) and **Obüs** (p105). Push onwards to Fitzroy's famed Brunswick St, the heartbeat of inner-north's bohemian spirit. Give your feet a break with strong espresso at **Marios** (p99), before exploring offbeat **Polyester Books** (p105).

☾ Still on Brunswick St head to **Naked for Satan's** (p100) rooftop bar for sensational views and predinner drinks and tapas. Head back to Gertrude St for your reservation at **Cutler & Co** (p99), followed by serious cocktails at the **Everleigh** (p100) or a 10-minute walk to the **Tote** (p102), one of Melbourne's most cherished live-music venues, to catch a gig or grab a stool at its divey front bar.

For a local's day in Fitzroy and Collingwood, see p94.

○ Local Life

Fitzroy & Collingwood Pub Crawl (p94)

Best of Melbourne

Shopping

Third Drawer Down (p103)

Gorman (p103)

Drinking

Naked for Satan (p100)

Everleigh (p100)

Panama Dining Room (p100)

Getting There

🚋 **Tram** 86 heads down Smith St, 112 along Brunswick St – both link to the city and St Kilda.

Local Life
Fitzroy & Collingwood Pub Crawl

All of the following pubs are local classics, and all housed within beautiful 19th-century brick buildings. Expect a welcoming laid-back crowd, rather than your 'too cool for school' crew. All have pub meals available for a pre-drink feed: highly advisable before setting out on this pub crawl.

....

❶ The Rose

A much-loved Fitzroy backstreet local, the **Rose** (406 Napier St, Fitzroy; ⏱ noon-midnight Sun-Wed, to 1am Thu-Sat; 🚌 86, 112) has remained true to its roots with cheap counter meals and an unpretentious local crowd who come to watch the footy.

❷ Little Creatures Dining Hall

The vast drinking hall at **Little Creatures** (📞 03-9417 5500; www.littlecreatures. au; 222 Brunswick St, Fitzroy;

8am-late; 📶; 🚌112) is the perfect place to imbibe beer from one of Australia's most successful microbreweries and gorge on pizzas.

❸ Labour in Vain

Boy's own beer barn, the **Labour in Vain** (📞03-9417 5955; www.labourinvain. com.au; 197a Brunswick St, Fitzroy; ⏰3pm-late Mon-Wed, 1pm-late Thu-Sun; 🚌112) has a pool table and lots of dingy period charm. Upstairs there's a deck perfect for lazy afternoons doing a spot of Brunswick St people-watching.

❹ The Standard

Flaunting a great beer garden, the **Standard** (📞03-9419 4793; 293 Fitzroy St, Fitzroy; ⏰3-11pm Mon & Tue, noon-11pm Wed-Sat, noon-9pm Sun; 🚌96, 112) is anything but its moniker. The Fitzroy backstreet local has down-to-earth bar staff, a truly eclectic crowd and an atmosphere defined by live music, footy on-screen, and loud and enthusiastic chatter.

❺ The Napier

The **Napier** (📞03-9419 4240; www. thenapierhotel.com; 210 Napier St, Fitzroy; ⏰3-11pm Mon-Thu, 1pm-1am Fri & Sat, 1-11pm Sun; 🚌86, 112) has stood on this corner for over a century; many beers have been pulled as the face of the neighbourhood changed. Worm your way around the central bar to the boisterous dining room for an iconic Bogan Burger. Head upstairs to check out the gallery, too.

❻ Union Club Hotel

A die-hard local, the **Union Club Hotel** (📞03-9417 2926; www.unionclubhotel.com. au; 164 Gore St, Collingwood; ⏰3pm-late Mon-Thu, noon-1am Fri-Sat, noon-11pm Sun; 🚌86) is swimming in earthy good vibes and happy chatter from the relaxed indie crowd. The large curved bar is one of Melbourne's best spots to park yourself, the food is honest pub nosh, and the beer garden and rooftop decking make for perfect lazing on a hot day.

❼ Grace Darling

The **Grace Darling** (www.gracedarling-hotel.com.au; 114 Smith St, Collingwood; 🚋86) has been given a bit of spit and polish by some well-known Melbourne foodies, and while the chicken parma remains, it is certainly not how you know it (more a terracotta bake of chargrilled chook, ham, slow-roasted tomato and parmesan). There's also live music, mainly aimed at the young indie crowd.

❽ Late-Night Snack

There's plenty of souvlaki and kebab joints open till early morning, but **Po' Boy Quarter** (295 Smith St, Fitzroy; rolls $9.90-12.90; ⏰11.30am-1am; 🚋86), the boys behind the Gumbo Kitchen truck, have parked permanently on Smith St with this smart canteen-style eatery. Wolf down a roll of pulled pork, shrimp with Louisiana hot sauce or fried green tomatoes with Cajun slaw.

Alexandra Pde (Eastern Hwy)

To Northcote
(3km)

400 m
0.25 miles

Westgarth St
Cecil St
Westgarth St
Rose St
Leicester St
Kerr St
Argyle St
Johnston St
Victoria St
Bell St
Moor St
King William St
Hanover St
Palmer St
Gertrude St
Victoria Pde

Nicholson St
Spring St
Fitzroy St
Brunswick St
Young St
Napier St
George St
Gore St
Smith St
Wellington St
Emerald St

Rose St
Kerr St
Chapel St
Greeves St
St David St
Moor St
Condell St
Charles St
Webb St

Centre for
Contemporary
Photography

Easey St
Sackville St
Johnston St
Perry St
Otter St
Vere St

Gallery
Gabrielle
Pizzi

COLLINGWOOD

Atherton
Reserve

FITZROY

Gertrude
Contemporary
Art Space

Little Victoria
St

Mahoney St
John St
Fitzroy St
Brunswick St
Kent St
Napier St
Gore St
Bedford St
Little Oxford St
Oxford St
Cambridge St
Wellington St
John St
Down St
Singleton St
Gipps St
Glasshouse Rd
Langridge St
Derby St
Mason St
Cambridge St
Wellington St
Rokeby St

Royal La
Fitzroy St
Brunswick St
Young St
Little Napier St
Napier St
Little George St
George St
Gore St
Little Smith St
Smith St
Peel St

Union Club Hotel (p95)

Sights

Gertrude Contemporary Art Space
GALLERY

 Map p96, B5

This nonprofit gallery and studio complex has been going strong for nearly 30 years; many of its alumni are now certified famous artists. The monthly openings are refreshingly come-as-you-are, with crowds often spilling onto the street, two-dollar wine in hand. (☑03-9419 3406; www. gertrude.org.au; 200 Gertrude St, Fitzroy; admission free; ⊙11am-5.30pm Tue-Fri, 11am-4.30pm Sat; ⬚86)

Centre for Contemporary Photography
GALLERY

2 ◉ Map p96, C2

This not-for-profit centre has a changing schedule of photography exhibitions across a couple of galleries. Shows traverse traditional technique and the highly conceptual. There's a particular fascination with work involving video projection, including a nightly after-hours screening in a window. Also offers photography courses. (CCP; ☑03-9417 1549; www.ccp. org.au; 404 George St, Fitzroy; admission free; ⊙11am-6pm Wed-Fri, noon-5pm Sat & Sun; ⬚86)

Gallery Gabrielle Pizzi GALLERY

 Map p96, A2

Gabrielle Pizzi, one of Australia's most respected dealers of Indigenous art, founded this gallery in the 1980s; her daughter Samantha continues to show contemporary city-based artists, as well as traditional artists from the communities of Balgo Hills, Papunya, Maningrida and the Tiwi Islands. (📞03-9416 4170; www.gabriellepizzi.com.

Local Life

Collingwood Arts Precinct

Quality galleries have long inhabited the gritty backstreets of Collingwood, and they've been consolidated as a **precinct** (www.collingwoodartsprecinct.com.au; 🚋86). The area includes contemporary works at the spacious **James Makin Gallery** (Map p96, D3; www.jamesmakingallery.com; 67 Cambridge St, Collingwood; ⏲11am-5pm Tue-Sun) and the intimate **Kick Gallery** (Map p96, C4; www.kickgallery.com; 4 Peel St, Collingwood); wonderful and affordable Indigenous art at **Mossenson** (Map p96, D5; www.mossensongalleries.com.au; 41 Derby St, Collingwood; ⏲10am-5pm Tue-Fri, 11am-5pm Sat); and a huge, varied collection at **Australian Galleries** (Map p96, C5; www.australiangalleries.com.au; 28 Derby St, Collingwood; ⏲10am-6pm). Most are closed Mondays and during January; visit the website for details.

---

au; 51 Victoria St, Fitzroy; admission free; ⏲10am-5pm Wed-Fri, noon-6pm Sat; 🚋11, 96, 112)

Eating

Moon Under Water MODERN AUSTRALIAN $$$

Another string to Andrew McConnell's bow is this whitewashed elegant dining room hidden away in the back of the Builders Arms Hotel (see 19 Map p96, C5). The set menu changes weekly and wine pairing comes at $55 extra per head. Vegetarian menus are available. If you prefer something more casual and à la carte, check out the adjoining bistro with its daily rotisserie menu (suckling pig) from 6pm. Bookings advised at least two weeks in advance. (📞03-9417 7700; www.buildersarmshotel.com.au; 211 Gertrude St, Fitzroy; 4-course set menu $75; ⏲6-10pm Wed-Sat, noon-3pm & 6-10pm Sun; 🚋86)

Gelato Messina ICE CREAM $

4 🍴 Map p96, C3

Newly opened Messina is hyped as Melbourne's best ice-creamery. Its popularity is evident in the long queues of hipsters waiting to wrap their smackers around smooth gelato like coconut and lychee, salted caramel and white chocolate, or pear and spiced rhubarb. (www.gelatomessina.com; 237 Smith St, Fitzroy; 1 scoop $4; ⏲noon-11pm Sun-Thu, to 11.30pm Fri & Sat; 🚋86)

Cutler & Co MODERN AUSTRALIAN $$$

5 Map p96, A4

Hyped for all the right reasons, this is one of Andrew McConnell's restaurants and though its decor might be a little over the top, its attentive, informed staff and joy-inducing dishes (including roast suckling pig, Earl Grey ice cream and moonlight bay oysters) have quickly made this one of Melbourne's best. (☏03-9419 4888; www.cutlerandco.com.au; 55 Gertrude St, Fitzroy; mains $39-47; ☺noon-late Fri & Sun, 6pm-late Mon-Thu; ☒86)

Jimmy Grants GREEK $

6 Map p96, C3

Set up by celebrity chef George Calombaris, this is not your ordinary souva joint – these are gourmet souvlakis, which you don't need to be plastered at 3am to enjoy. Options may include a pita stuffed with lamb, mustard aioli and chips, or honey prawn and herbs. (www.jimmygrants.com. au; 113 St David St, Fitzroy; souvlakis from $9; ☺11am-10pm; ☒86)

Commoner MODERN BRITISH $$$

7 Map p96, B2

On a mission to dispel the myth that British food is dull, the Commoner succeeds with a sensational highly seasonal menu that incorporates classic ingredients into creative dishes. Think pork belly with black pudding, broccoli and anchovy, a side of chicken-skin potatoes, and brown-ale pudding with salted-caramel sauce

and cream for dessert. Sunday lunches are all about its wood-fired roast goat or beef. (☏03-9415 6876; www.thecommoner.com.au; 122 Johnston St, Fitzroy; mains from $30, 5-course menu $70; ☺noon-3pm Fri-Sun, 6pm-late Wed-Sun; ☒112)

Huxtaburger BURGERS $

8 Map p96, C4

This American-style burger joint is a hipster magnet for its crinkle-cut chips in old-school containers, tasty burgers (veg options available) on glazed brioche buns and bottled craft beers. Cash only. Other branches can be found in the City and Prahran. (☏03-9417 6328; www.huxtaburger.com. au; 106 Smith St, Collingwood; burgers from $8.50; ☺11.30am-10pm Sun-Thu, to 11pm Fri & Sat; ☒86)

Marios CAFE $$

9 Map p96, B2

Mooching at Marios is part of the Melbourne 101 curriculum. Breakfasts are big and served all day, the service is swift, dishes are simple classic Italian and the coffee is old-school strong. (www.marioscafe.com.au; 303 Brunswick St, Fitzroy; mains $17-30; ☺7am-10.30pm Mon-Sat, 8am-10.30pm Sun; ☒112)

Charcoal Lane MODERN AUSTRALIAN $$

10 Map p96, B5

Housed in an old bluestone former bank, this training restaurant for Indigenous and disadvantaged young people is one of the best places to try native flora and fauna; menu items may include kangaroo burger with bush tomato chutney and wallaby tartare. Weekend bookings advised. Also holds cooking masterclasses using native ingredients; check the website for details. (☑03-9418 3400; www.charcoallane.com.au; 136 Gertrude St, Fitzroy; mains $28-35; ☺noon-3pm & 6-9pm Tue-Sat; ⌂86)

Vegie Bar
VEGETARIAN $$

11 Map p96, B1

The menu of delicious thin-crust pizzas, tasty curries and seasonal broths is perfectly suited to the cavernous warehouse decor with walls covered in band posters. Also has a fascinating selection of raw food dishes, and plenty of vegan choices. Its fresh juices are popular, as are its yummy, cheap and original breakfasts. (☑03-9417 6935; www.vegiebar.com.au; 380 Brunswick St, Fitz-

---

Local Life
Rosamond

Just off Smith St, the tiny **Rosamond** (Map p96, C4 ☑03-9419 2270; 191 Smith St, Fitzroy; dishes $5-12; ☺7.30am-3.15pm Mon-Fri, from 9am Sat; ⌂86) is a warm haven for the local freelance creative crew who like their daily rations simple but well considered. And that they are: free-range eggs only come scrambled, but with first-rate toast and fresh sides, and there's soup, toasties, baguettes, salads and cupcakes.

---

roy; mains $14-16; ☺11am-10.30pm Mon-Fri, from 9am Sat & Sun; ✈; ⌂112)

Drinking

Naked for Satan
BAR

12 Map p96, B2

Vibrant, loud and reviving an apparent Brunswick St legend (a man nicknamed Satan who would get down and dirty, naked because of the heat, in an illegal vodka distillery under the shop), this place packs a punch with its popular *pintxos* (Basque tapas; $2), huge range of cleverly named beverages and unbeatable roof terrace with wraparound decked balcony. (☑03-9416 2238; www.nakedforsatan.com.au; 285 Brunswick St, Fitzroy; ☺noon-12am Sun-Thu, to 1am Fri & Sat; ⌂112)

Everleigh
COCKTAIL BAR

13 Map p96, B5

Sophistication and bartending standards are off the charts at this upstairs hidden nook. Settle into a leather booth in the intimate setting with a few friends for conversation and oohing-and-ahhing over classic 'golden era' cocktails like you've never tasted before. (www.theeverleigh.com; 150-156 Gertrude St, Fitzroy; ☺5.30pm-late; ⌂86)

Panama Dining Room
BAR

14 Map p96, C3

Gawp at the ersatz Manhattan views in this large warehouse-style space

Marios (p99)

while sipping serious cocktails and snacking on truffled polenta chips or falafel balls with tahini. The dining area gets packed around 9pm for its Mod European menu. (☎03-9417 7663; www.thepanama.com.au; 3rd fl, 231 Smith St, Fitzroy; 🚊86)

De Clieu

CAFE

15 🚇 Map p96, B5

You'll find locals spilling out the door and perched on the window-sill seats on weekends at funky cafe De Clieu (pronounced 'clue') with its polished concrete floors and excellent coffee, courtesy of Seven Seeds. The all-day brunch menu features interesting cafe

fare such as miso and broad-bean fritters, scrambled tofu and pork-neck roti. (187 Gertrude St, Fitzroy; ⏰7am-5pm Mon-Sat, 8am-5pm Sun; 🚊86)

Proud Mary

CAFE

16 🚇 Map p96, D3

A champion for direct-trade, single-origin coffee; caffeine is serious business here at what is your quintessential backstreet industrial Collingwood red-brick space, regularly packed out with hipsters woofing down green eggs on toast or crispy pork belly sandwiches. (☎03-9417 5930; 172 Oxford St, Collingwood; ⏰7.30am-4pm Mon-Fri, 8.30am-4pm Sat & Sun; 🛜, 🚊86)

Industry Beans

CAFE

17 Map p96, A2

It's all about coffee chemistry at this warehouse cafe tucked in a Fitzroy side street. The coffee guide takes you through the specialty styles on offer (roasted on site) and helpful staff take the pressure off deciding. Pair your brew with some latte coffee pearls or coffee toffee prepared in the 'lab'. The food menu is ambitious but doesn't always hit the mark. (www.industrybeans. com; cnr Fitzroy & Rose Sts, Fitzroy; ⏰7am-4pm Mon-Fri, 8am-5pm Sat & Sun; 🛜; 🚊96, 112)

Bar Open

BAR

18 Map p96, B2

This long-established bar, as the name suggests, is often open when everything else is closed. The bar attracts a relaxed young local crowd ready to kick on. Bands play in the upstairs loft Tuesday to Friday and are almost always free. (☎03-9415 9601; www. baropen.com.au; 317 Brunswick St, Fitzroy; ⏰3pm-late; 🚊112)

Builders Arms Hotel

PUB

19 Map p96, C5

A completely re-imagined bad old boozer, the Builders Arms has retained its charm despite theatrical new threads. Come for a pot of beer by all means, but there's also decent wine and popular char-grilled meat barbecues. Picnic-style tables streetside are perfect for taking in Gertrude St. (☎03-9417 7700; www.buildersarmshotel.

Top Tip

Northcote

If you enjoy Collingwood's vibe, stay on tram 86 for a short ride up to High St, Northcote, for more band venues, cool cafes, restaurants and designer shops.

com.au; 211 Gertrude St, Fitzroy; ⏰noon-late Mon-Fri, from 11am Sat & Sun; 🚊86)

Entertainment

The Tote

LIVE MUSIC

20 Map p96, D3

One of Melbourne's most iconic live-music venues, not only does this divey Collingwood pub have a great roster of local and international underground bands, but one of the best jukeboxes in the universe. Its temporary closure in 2010 brought Melbourne to a stop, literally – people protested on the city-centre streets against the liquor licensing laws that were blamed for the closure. (☎03-9419 5320; www.the-totehotel.com; cnr Johnston & Wellington Sts, Collingwood; ⏰4pm-late Tue-Sun; 🚊86)

Old Bar

LIVE MUSIC, PUB

21 Map p96, A2

With live bands seven days a week and a license till 3am, the Old Bar's another reason why Melbourne is the rock 'n' roll capital of Australia. It gets great local bands and a few internationals playing in its grungy bandroom with a house-party vibe. (☏ 03-9417 4155; www.theoldbar.com.au; 74-76 Johnston St, Fitzroy; 🛜; 🚃 96, 112)

Night Cat
LIVE MUSIC, BAR

22 ⭐ Map p96, B2

The Night Cat is a barn-sized space that saw the birth of the upside-down lampshade aesthetic in the mid-'90s. There are two bars, a stage and a black-and-white chequered dance floor that sees lots of action. Music is generally in the Latin, jazz or funk vein. Offers salsa dance classes ($15) on Sunday nights (☏ 03-9417 0090; www. thenightcat.com.au; 141 Johnston St, Fitzroy; ⊙ 9pm-3am Fri-Sat, 7pm-3am Sun; 🚃 112)

Shopping

Third Drawer Down
DESIGN

23 🔒 Map p96, B4

It all started with the signature tea-towel designs (now found in MOMA in New York) at this 'museum of art souvenirs'. Third Drawer Down makes life beautifully unusual by stocking absurdist pieces with a sense of humour as well as high-end art by well-known designers. (www.thirddrawerdown.com; 93 George St, Fitzroy; ⊙ 11am-5pm Mon-Sat; 🚃 86)

Gorman
CLOTHING, ACCESSORIES

24 🔒 Map p96, B3

Lisa Gorman makes everyday clothes that are far from ordinary: boyish,

but sexy, short shapes are cut from exquisite fabrics; pretty cardigans are coupled with relaxed, organic tees. You can find other branches elsewhere around town. (www.gormanshop. com.au; 235 Brunswick St, Fitzroy; ⊙ 10am-6pm Mon-Thu & Sat, to 7pm Fri, 11am-5pm Sun; 🚃 112)

Aesop
BEAUTY

25 🔒 Map p96, C5

This homegrown empire specialises in citrus-and-botanical based aromatic balms, hair masques, scents, cleansers and oils in beautifully simple packaging for both men and women. There are plenty of branches around town (and plenty of opportunity to sample the products in most of Melbourne's cafe bathrooms). (www.aesop.com; 242 Gertrude St, Fitzroy; ⊙ 11am-5pm Mon & Sun, 10am-6pm Tue-Fri, 10am-5pm Sat; 🚃 86)

Books for Cooks
BOOKS

26 🔒 Map p96, C5

The breadth of this shop's new and secondhand collection is astounding, ranging from obscure gastronomic histories and books on Indigenous

 Top Tip

Keith Haring Mural
On Johnston St (next door to the Tote) look out for a mural painted by the late Keith Haring, the famous New York street artist, who visited in 1984.

GERARD WALKER / GETTY IMAGES ©

Crumpler

and bush tucker recipes to the latest celeb chef how-to. Extremely knowledgeable staff will help you find whatever you're after. (www. booksforcooks.com.au; 233-235 Gertrude St, Fitzroy; ⏰10am-6pm Mon-Sat, 11am-5pm Sun; 🚊86)

Mud Australia

CERAMICS

27 🔒 Map p96, B5

You'll find some of the most aesthetically beautiful – as well as functional – porcelain ware from Australian-designed Mud. Coffee mugs, milk pourers, salad bowls and serving plates come in muted pastel colours with a raw matte finish. Prices start from $20 per piece. (www.

mudaustralia.com; 181 Gertrude St, Fitzroy; ⏰10am-6pm Mon-Fri, 11am-6pm Sat, noon-5pm Sun; 🚊86)

Ess

CLOTHING

28 🔒 Map p96, B5

Japanese design duo Hoshika Oshimie and her sound-artist collaborative partner Tatsuyoshi Kawabata have created waves in Melbourne since Hoshika established Ess Laboratory in 2001. The National Gallery of Victoria has Ess designs in its gallery collection; but don't let that stop you claiming one for yourself. (www.ess-laboratory. com; 114 Gertrude St, Fitzroy; ⏰11am-5.30pm Mon, 10.30am-6pm Tue-Fri, 10am-5.30pm Sat, 1-5pm Sun; 🚊86)

Obüs

FASHION

29 Map p96, C5

Melbourne-based designer Kylie Zerbst set up Obüs 15 years ago with this, her first store. Known for bright geometric patterns and soft bamboo-cotton travel essentials, the clothing is sophisticated yet fun and offers pieces that get you from work to going out without a change. Other branches located at QV in the city and in Northcote. (www.obus.com.au; 226 Gertrude St, Fitzroy; 10am-6pm Mon-Sat, noon-5pm Sun; 86)

Crumpler

ACCESSORIES

30 Map p96, C5

Crumpler's bike-courier bags started it all, designed by two former couriers looking for a bag they could hold their beer in while cycling home. Its durable, practical designs now extend to bags for cameras, laptops and iPods, and can be found around the world. (03-9417 5338; www.crumpler.com; 87 Smith St, cnr Gertrude St, Fitzroy; 10am-6pm Mon-Sat, to 5pm Sun; 86)

Local Life

Rose Street Artists' Market

One of Melbourne's most popular art-and-craft markets, **Rose Street** (Map p96, A1; www.rosestmarket.com.au; 60 Rose St, Fitzroy; 11am-5pm Sat; 112) showcases the best of local designers, just a short stroll from Brunswick St. Here you'll find up to 70 stalls selling matte silver jewellery, clothing, milk-bottle ceramics, iconic Melbourne screen prints, wild fig candles and ugly-cute toys. Humble Vintage has bike-hire available here.

Polyester Books

BOOKS

31 Map p96, B2

This unapologetic bookstore specialises in 'seriously weird shit', including literature, magazines and DVDs on topics ranging from satanic cult sex to underground comics and everything in between. It also stocks a great selection of music biographies and small-press zines. (03-9419 5223; www.polyester.com.au; 330 Brunswick St, Fitzroy; 10am-6pm, to 9pm Fri & Sat; 112)

Top Sights
Abbotsford Convent & Around

Getting There

🚗 Head east down Johnston St, turn right at Clarke St then left into Heliers St.

🚌 200, 201, 207

🚉 Collingwood, Victoria Park

The nuns are long gone at this former convent, which dates back to 1861, so don't worry, no one will ask if you've been to Mass lately. Today its rambling collection of ecclesiastic architecture is home to a thriving arts community of galleries, studios, cafes and bars, spread over nearly 7 hectares of riverside land. The adjoining Collingwood Children's Farm has a range of frolicking farm animals that kids can help feed, while Yarra Bend Park makes for a lovely scenic bike ride or walk.

Convent Bakery

Don't Miss

Theatre & Cinema

Offbeat **Kage Physical Theatre** (☑03-9417 6700;
www.kagephysicaltheatre.com) offers witty and innovative modern dance performances. The **Shadow
Electric** (www.shadowelectric.com.au) open-air
cinema screens cult classics from November to
March and has a popular bar with ping-pong.

Markets

The convent is home to a number of markets.
The **Shirt & Skirt Market** (www.shirtandskirtmarkets.
com.au) on the third Sunday of each month is the
place to buy limited-run clothes and accessories
from emerging designers. There's the **Slow Food
Market** every fourth Saturday, and in summer the
popular **Supper Market** on Friday nights, featuring food stalls and live music.

Collingwood Children's Farm

The inner city melts away at rustic, riverside
Collingwood Children's Farm (www.farm.org.au;
18 St Heliers St, Abbotsford; adult/child/family $8/4/16;
☺9am-4.30pm), a retreat that's beloved not just by
kids. As well as farm animals to help feed, there
are rambling gardens and grounds for picnicking
on warm days. The monthly farmers market is a
local highlight.

Yarra Bend Park

Backing onto the convent, the Yarra River flows
through scenic bushland with plenty of birdlife,
great walking, cycling and picnicking. At the end
of Boathouse Rd, Studley Park Boathouse, accessed via suspension footbridge across the river,
has a kiosk, restaurant, BBQs and canoes for hire.

☑03-9415 3600

www.abbotsford-
convent.com.au

1 St Heliers St,
Abbotsford

☺7.30am-10pm

☑ Top Tips

▶ Tours ($15) of the
complex are run at 2pm
every Sunday.

▶ Car parking is re-
stricted, not to mention
pricey, so catch public
transport, or cycle along
Yarra Bend bike path.

✗ Take a Break

Plenty of great foodie
options here. Try not-for-
profit **Lentil as Anything**
(www.lentilasanything.
com; by donation; ☺9am-
9pm; ☑) for delicious
vegetarian dishes and
the **Convent Bakery**
(www.conventbakery.com;
☺7am-5pm), which bakes
goodies in the original
1901 wood-fired ma-
sonry ovens.

Explore

Carlton & Around

Carlton is the heartland of Melbourne's Italian community. It's most known for Lygon St, with its abundance of trattorias and espresso cafes, and come the Grand Prix and soccer finals you'll see the *tricolori* (Italian flag) unfurled with characteristic passion. Carlton's home to prestigious Melbourne Uni, and surrounded by leafy North Carlton, up-and-coming North Melbourne and hip East Brunswick.

The Sights in a Day

☀ Coffee drinkers are spoilt for choice in this area. For your morning brew head to **Auction Rooms** (p119) or **Seven Seeds** (p119), both regarded among the city's finest roasters. Otherwise head to Lygon St for traditional espresso at **Tiamo** (p118), one of Lygon St's originals. While you're here duck into **Museo Italiano** (p116) to get informed on the area's Italian history.

☀ After a lunch of authentic thin-crust pizza from **DOC Pizzeria** (p117), start your afternoon of sightseeing at Australia's oldest **zoo** (p116), established in 1862. Catch a tram towards the city to Nicholson St to admire the World Heritage–listed **Royal Exhibition Building** (p112), a striking art nouveau gem. Next door is the impressive **Melbourne Museum** (p110), which has a varied and accessible collection, including good coverage on Indigenous Australia.

☽ Return to Lygon St and **DOC Espresso** (p117) for a Negroni *aperitivo* and complimentary snacks. For dinner, move away from Italian for a Lebanese meal at **Abla's** (p118) or some French at **Aux Batifolles** (p118) before enjoying quality indie theatre at **La Mama** (p120) or art-house flicks and a choc-top ice cream at **Cinema Nova** (p121).

 Top Sights

Melbourne Museum (p110)

Royal Exhibition Building (p112)

♥ **Best of Melbourne**

Eating
DOC Espresso (p117)

Tiamo (p118)

Abla's (p118)

Drinking
Seven Seeds (p119)

Auction Rooms (p119)

Getting There

🚋 **Tram** City Circle, 1, 8, 19, 55, 57, 59, 86, 96

🚌 **Bus** Tourist Shuttle, 205

🚆 **Train** Parliament Station for Melbourne Museum and Royal Exhibition Building; Royal Park for Melbourne Zoo

Top Sights
Melbourne Museum

The Melbourne Museum provides a grand sweep of Victoria's natural and cultural histories, with exhibitions covering everything from dinosaur fossils and giant squid specimens to a blue whale skeleton, a 3-D volcano and an open-air forest atrium of Victorian flora. Become immersed in the history of Melbourne and the legend of champion racehorse and national hero Phar Lap in the *Melbourne Story* exhibition. The excellent Bunjilaka, on the ground floor, is a must-see and there's also an IMAX cinema on-site.

◉ Map p114, G5

www.museumvictoria.com.au

11 Nicholson St, Carlton

adult/child & student $10/free, exhibitions extra

⊙ 10am-5pm

🚌 Tourist Shuttle, 🚃 City Circle, 86, 96, 🚇 Parliament

Bunjilaka Aboriginal Culture Centre

Don't Miss

Bunjilaka Aboriginal Cultural Centre

The *First Peoples* permanent exhibition at the Bunjilaka Aboriginal Cultural Centre presents Indigenous Australian stories and history told through objects and Aboriginal voices with state-of-the-art technology. Highlights of the exhibition include the traditional possum skin cloaks, Bunjil's wings – a kinetic sculptural audiovisual installation – and the Deep Listening space, where you can hear Koorie people speak about their culture and share personal stories.

Taxidermy Hall

This impressive hall houses a large number of taxidermied animals set over different levels and you can peer down on them all from above. Here you can see Sam the Koala, who made headlines after footage was released of a firefighter giving her water and rescuing her during the devastating 2009 Black Saturday bushfires. She died afterwards and became the symbol of the loss from the fires.

Melbourne Gallery

The permanent *Melbourne Story* exhibition features around 1200 objects that help you delve into the city's history and get a sense of its personality. Walk through the history of Little Lonsdale St and check out the schoolboy costume of Angus Young of famous Australian rock band AC/DC. In this gallery you'll also find the museum's most popular display, the taxidermied Phar Lap, Australia's national hero and most loved racehorse of all time.

☑ **Top Tips**

▶ Avoid queues by buying your tickets online in advance on the museum website.

▶ Join a free guided tour of the museum's highlights; ask for the schedule as times can change daily.

▶ You'll need at least half a day to explore the museum.

▶ If you plan on visiting the IMAX theatre next door, buy a combined ticket at the museum for a discount.

✗ **Take a Break**

The most convenient option for a quick bite is the museum's on-site cafe on the ground floor, though it can get busy on weekends and holidays. Otherwise head to the ultracontemporary space of Assembly (p119) cafe, a 10-minute walk away, for speciality filtered coffee and artisan teas complemented by delicious pastries.

Top Sights
Royal Exhibition Building

Built for the International Exhibition in 1880 and winning Unesco World Heritage status in 2004, this beautiful Victorian edifice symbolises the glory days of the Industrial Revolution, the British Empire and 19th-century Melbourne's economic supremacy. It was the first building to fly the Australian flag, and Australia's first parliament was held here in 1901; it now hosts everything from trade fairs to car shows.

👁 Map p114, G5

www.museumvictoria.com.au/reb

9 Nicholson St, Carlton

tours adult/child $5/3.50

🚋 Tourist Shuttle,
🚋 City Circle, 86, 96,
🚆 Parliament

Don't Miss

The Architecture

Designed by architect Joseph Reed, the stunning Royal Exhibition Building is the only surviving Great Hall that was originally used for a 19th-century international exhibition and is still used for the same purpose to this day. Admire the round-arched Rundbogenstil architecture, a style which combines elements from Romanesque, Lombardic, Byzantine and Italian Renaissance buildings. The design of the dome was influenced by Brunelleschi's 15th-century cathedral in Florence. In 2004 the Royal Exhibition Building became the first building in Australia to be given World Heritage listing.

The Interior

The inside of the building is as impressive as the exterior, with extensive decorative paintwork throughout and exquisite detail. In the spaces where the arches join the cornices, you can see intricate lunettes with sculptural details that represent Peace, War, Federation and Government. The interior underwent a massive restoration project in 1994 to bring it back to its 1901 colour scheme.

Carlton Gardens

The surrounding gardens, also part of the World Heritage listing, are a popular, peaceful spot for nearby office workers, locals and tourists. The gardens are bordered by Victoria, Rathdowne, Carlton and Nicholson Sts, and are a great example of Victorian landscaping with a network of wide tree-lined avenues, a beautiful fountain and native wildlife.

☑ Top Tips

▶ The only way to see inside is by tour or on entry to an exhibition.

▶ Tours ($5) of the building run most days, leaving Melbourne Museum at 2pm.

▶ The building hosts the biennial Melbourne Art Fair in August, Australasia's leading contemporary art event.

✕ Take a Break

Pack some picnic goodies before you set off: the surrounding Carlton Gardens provide the perfect spot for a lunchtime break. For something a bit more upmarket, try nearby **Epocha** (☏ 03-9036 4949; www.epocha. com.au; 49 Rathdowne St, Carlton; sharing plates small/large from $14/24; ⊘ noon-2pm & 5.30-10pm Tue-Sat; ☐ City Circle, 24, 30). Set within a grand Victorian 1884 double-storey terrace, it creates an interesting mix of Greek- and English-inspired dishes reflective of the co-owners' successes in previous restaurants.

A B C D

Royal Melbourne Zoo

Brunswick (1.5km)

N

0   500 m
0   0.25 miles

Brens Dr

Elliot Ave

The Avenue

Royal Park

Macarthur Rd

PARKVILLE

Racecourse Rd

Elliott Ave

Royal Park

Boundary Rd

Alfred St

Flemington Rd

Sutton St

Curran St

Bruce St

Melrose St

Gatehouse St

Fitzgibbon St

Royal Pde

Royal Children's Hospital

Erskine St

Dryburgh St

Chapman St

Park Dr

Morrah St

Canning St

Harker St

Story St

Macaulay Rd

Shiel St

Wood St

Molesworth St

Flemington Rd

3
Grainger Museum

North Melbourne Cricket Ground

Fogarty St

Gardiner Reserve

Haines St

NORTH MELBOURNE

Harris St

O'Shanassy St

Errol St

Murphy St

Harcourt St

Villiers St

Royal Melbourne Hospital

Grattan St

Arden St

Laurens St

Lothian St

Baillie St

Provost St

Curzon St

9

Arden St

Byron St

Wrecklyn St

Courtney St

Blackwood St

O'Connell St

Elizabeth

Queensberry St

Elm St

Errol St

Leveson St

Chetwynd St

Howard St

Capel St

Peel St

King St

Victoria St

Victoria St

For reviews see	
◉ Top Sights	p110
◎ Sights	p116
✕ Eating	p117
✕ Drinking	p119
★ Entertainment	p120
🔒 Shopping	p121

E

F

G

H

Princes
Park

**CARLTON
NORTH**

Fenwick St

**FITZROY
NORTH**

1

Church St

Princes Park Dr

Lygon St

Drummond St

Rathdowne St

Nicholson St

St Georges Rd

Curtain St

Curtain
Square

Newry St

🔒 **18**

Rae St

*Melbourne
General
Cemetery*

metery
d W

◎ **4**

College Cres

Canning St

8

⊗

Lee St

York St

2

Davis St

Cemetery Rd
E

Princes St

**Alexandra Pde
(Eastern Hwy)**

Cecil St

Swanston St

Cardigan St

Lygon St

Neill St

Canning St

Westgarth St

Rose St

Fitzroy St

3

Tin Alley

Elgin St

14

Kay St

Pitt St

Palmerston St

Nicholson St

Kerr St

Brunswick St

Ian Potter
Museum ◎
of Art

2

12 📍

20 🔒

Drummond St

Rathdowne St

Elgin St

Argyle St

Johnston St

Monash Rd

6 ⊗

Faraday St

⊗ **7**

**Macarthur
Square**

Victoria St

*University of
Melbourne*

☆ **16**

⊗ **5**

Faraday St

Greeves St

Barkly St

Murchison
Square

Bell St

4

🔒 **19**

*University
Square*

Grattan St

Owen St

Carlton St

FITZROY

CARLTON

Carlton
Gardens
North

Moor St

Lincoln
Square

Argyle
Square

11

*Melbourne
Museum* ◎

King William St

Leicester St

Bouverie St

Swanston St

Cardigan St

Lygon St

Drummond St

Rathdowne St

📍

☆
17

Nicholson St

Hanover St

Brunswick St

5

🔒 **13**

Grattan St

*Royal
Exhibition
Building* ◎

Palmer St

Queensberry St

Fitzroy St

Gertrude St

**RMIT
University**

15 ☆

Carlton
Gardens
South

Sights

Royal Melbourne Zoo
ZOO

1 Map p114, C1

Established in 1862, this is the oldest zoo in Australia and the third-oldest in the world. Today it's one of the city's most popular attractions. Set in spacious, prettily landscaped gardens, the zoo's enclosures aim to simulate the animals' natural habitats. Walkways pass through the enclosures: you can stroll through the bird aviary, cross a bridge over the lions' park or enter a tropical hothouse full of colourful butterflies. (☑03-9285 9300; www.zoo.org.au; Elliott Ave, Parkville; adult/child $30/13.20, children free on weekends & holidays; �is9am-5pm; ☒505, ☒55, ☒Royal Park)

Ian Potter Museum of Art
GALLERY

2 Map p114, E3

Part of Melbourne University, the Ian Potter Museum of Art manages the

Local Life
Museo Italiano

Telling the story of Melbourne's Italian community, **Museo Italiano** (Map p114, F4; ☑03-9349 9000; www.museoitaliano.com.au; 199 Faraday St, Carlton; admission free; �is10am-5pm Tue-Fri, noon-5pm Sat) offers a good starting point to put the history of Lygon St into both historical and contemporary context.

university's extensive art collection, which ranges from antiquities to contemporary Australian work. It's a thoughtfully designed space and always has an exciting exhibition program. Pick up the *Sculpture on Campus* map here for a walking tour around Melbourne Uni's sculptures, set amid heritage-listed buildings. (www.art-museum.unimelb.edu.au; 800 Swanston St, Carlton; admission free; �is10am-5pm Tue-Fri, noon-5pm Sat & Sun; ☒6, 8, 72)

Grainger Museum
MUSEUM

3 Map p114, D3

A tribute to one of Australia's great musical exports, Percy Grainger's fascinating life is laid bare within this art deco building. Leaving Australia as a nine-year-old, Grainger became an internationally renowned composer and pianist in Europe and the USA, as well a forerunner in experimental music. Exhibits from all points of his extraordinary life are on display, from his sound machines to collection of fetish whips. (☑03-8344 5270; www.grainger.unimelb.edu.au; Gate 13, Melbourne Uni, Royal Pde, Parkville; admission free; �is1-4.30pm Tue-Fri & Sun, closed Jan; ☒19)

Melbourne General Cemetery
CEMETERY

4 Map p114, F2

Melbourne has been burying its dead in this cemetery since 1852. It's worth a stroll to see the final resting place

RICHARD I'ANSON / GETTY IMAGES ©

Melbourne General Cemetery

of three Australian prime ministers, the ill-fated explorers Burke and Wills, Walter Lindrum's billiard-table tombstone and a shrine to Elvis erected by fans. Check the website about night-time tours. (☑03-9349 3014; www.mgc.smct.org.au; College Cres, Parkville; ◷9am-5pm; 🚋1, 8)

Eating

DOC Espresso
ITALIAN $$

5 ✕ Map p114, F4

Run by third-generation Italians, DOC is bringing authenticity, and breathing new life, back into Lygon St. The espresso bar features homemade pasta specials, Italian microbrewery beers and *aperitivo* time, where you can enjoy a Negroni cocktail with complimentary nibble board (4pm to 7pm) while surrounded by dangling legs of meat and huge wheels of cheese behind glass shelves.

The **deli** (◷9am-8pm) next door does great cheese boards and panini, while around the corner is the original **pizzeria** (☑03-9347 2998; 295 Drummond St; pizzas around $13-18; ◷5.30-10.30pm Mon-Thu, noon-10.30pm Fri-Sun), with excellent thin-crust pizzas and a convivial atmosphere. (☑03-9347 8482; www.docgroup.net; 326 Lygon St, Carlton; mains $12-20; ◷7.30am-9.30pm

Jimmy Watson's

Mon-Thu, to 10pm Fri & Sat, 8am-10pm Sun; 📮205, 🚋1, 8, 96)

Tiamo
ITALIAN **$$**

6 Map p114, F4

When you've had enough of pressed, siphoned, Slayer-machined, poured-over, filtered and plunged coffee, head here to one of Lygon St's original Italian cafe-restaurants. There's the laughter and relaxed *joie de vivre* that only a well-established restaurant can have. Great pastas and pizza, too. Also has the upmarket Tiamo 2 next door. (www.tiamo.com.au; 303 Lygon St, Carlton; mains $9-24; ⏱6.30am-11pm; 📮Tourist Shuttle, 🚋1, 8)

Abla's
LEBANESE **$$**

7 Map p114, G3

The kitchen here is steered by Abla Amad, whose authentic, flavour-packed food has inspired a whole generation of local Lebanese chefs. Bring a bottle of your favourite plonk and settle in for the compulsory banquet ($70) on Friday and Saturday night. (☑03-9347 0006; www. ablas.com.au; 109 Elgin St, Carlton; mains $27; ⏱noon-3pm Thu & Fri, 6-11pm Mon-Sat; 📮205, 🚋1, 8, 96)

Aux Batifolles
FRENCH **$$**

8 Map p114, H2

In the evenings this atmospheric French bistro does alll the classics: duck *confit, moules frites* (mussels and French fries), frog legs and steak tartare. Desserts too: crème brûlée and *tarte Tatin* (upside-down tart). During the day it's a fabulous cafe that does homemade baguettes and croissants, and well-priced traditional steaks and chicken dishes for lunch. (☑03-9481 5015; www.auxbatifolles.

✅ Top Tip

Lygon Street Eats

When looking for dining spots, avoid Carlton's Lygon St spruikers and keep travelling north past Grattan St, where you'll find some lovely cafes and restaurants.

com.au; 400 Nicholson St, North Fitzroy; breakfast/lunch/dinner from $7.50/12/26; ⏱cafe 8am-2.30pm Wed-Sun, restaurant 6-9.30pm Tue-Sat; 🚊96)

Auction Rooms
CAFE $$

9 Map p114, C4

This former auction house turned North Melbourne success story serves up some of Melbourne's best coffee, both espresso and filter, using ever-changing, house-roasted single-origin beans. Then there's the food, with a highly seasonal menu of creative breakfasts and lunches. From Queen Victoria Market head west along Victoria St, then right at Errol. (www.auctionroomscafe.com.au; 103-107 Errol St, North Melbourne; mains $14-20; ⏱7am-5pm Mon-Fri, from 7.30am Sat & Sun; 🛜; 🚊57)

Drinking

Seven Seeds
CAFE

10 Map p114, E5

The most spacious of the Seven Seeds coffee empire; there's plenty of room to store your bike and sip a splendid coffee beside the other lucky people who've found this rather out-of-the-way warehouse cafe. Public cuppings (tastings) are held Wednesday (9am) and Saturday (10am). There's also standing-room only Traveller and Brother Baba Budan (p41). (www.sevenseeds.com.au; 114 Berkeley St, Carlton; ⏱7am-5pm Mon-Sat, 8am-5pm Sun; 🚊19, 59)

Top Tip

Get Active

Joggers and walkers pound the 3.2km gravel path around the perimeter of **Princes Park** (Map p114, E1; Princes Park Dr, North Carlton; 🚊19), while cricket, soccer and dog-walking fill up the centre. It's also the current training ground of the Carlton Football Club. **Royal Park** (Map p114, C2; btwn Royal Pde & Flemington Rd, Parkville) has vast open spaces perfect for a run or power walk, plus sports ovals, netball and hockey stadiums, a golf course and tennis courts. In the northwestern section of the park, Trin Warren Tam-boore is a recently established wetlands area, with boardwalks and interpretive signs for spotting native plants and animals.

Assembly
CAFE

11 Map p114, F4

A far departure from what coffee once meant to Lygon St, you won't find an espresso machine here. Rather, Assembly is all about filter coffee with single-origin beans, plus an artisanal tea selection, all matched with Matt Forbes' pastries. (www.assemblystore.com; 60 Pelham St, Carlton; ⏱8am-5pm Mon-Fri, from 10am Sat & Sun; 🛜; 🚊1, 8)

Jimmy Watson's
WINE BAR

12 Map p114, F3

Keep it tidy at Watson's wine bar with something nice by the glass, or go a bottle of dry and dry (vermouth and ginger ale) and settle in for the afternoon and evening. If this Robyn Boyd–designed stunning midcentury building had ears, there'd be a few generations of writers, students and academics in trouble. (📞03-9347 3985; www.jimmywatsons.com.au; 333 Lygon St, Carlton; ⏱11am-11pm; 🚃1, 8)

Stovetop
CAFE

13 🚇 Map p114, E5

Just up from the Vic Market, Stovetop lives up to its name by preparing and serving its house blend and single-origins in stovetop espresso makers. Order from its bar set on 1970s Besser concrete blocks, and grab a gourmet sausage roll, Gruyère cheese toastie with chutney or baked duck eggs for brekkie. (www.stovetop.com.au; 100 Leices-

Local Life
Town Hall Hotel

The **Town Hall** (Map p114, C5; 📞03-9328 1983; www.townhallhotelnorth-melbourne.com.au; 33 Errol St, North Melbourne; ⏱4pm-1am Mon-Thu, noon-1am Fri & Sat, noon-11pm Sun; 🚃57) is an unfussy local with a beer garden and pub meals. Live music is staged free in the front room from Thursday to Saturday, and at other times there'll be some classic vinyl spinning. From the Queen Vic Market, head west along Victoria St, then right at Errol St.

ter St, Carlton; ⏱7am-5pm Mon-Fri, 8am-4pm Sat & Sun; 🛜; 🚃19, 57, 59)

Campos Coffee
CAFE

14 🚇 Map p114, G3

A Slayer espresso machine, pour-overs, aeropress, siphon, 22-hour cold-drips, on-site roasting, cupping and daily-changing single-origin African, Asia and Latin American coffees – Campos has it all covered for the modern-day caffeine freak. (www.camposcoffee.com; 144 Elgin St, Carlton; ⏱7am-4pm Mon-Fri, from 8am Sat; 🚃1, 8)

Entertainment

John Curtin Hotel
LIVE MUSIC, PUB

15 ⭐ Map p114, F5

Popular with uni students, the John Curtin is a great pub for a beer; it also hosts some great local indie and rock bands upstairs most nights. (📞03-9663 6350; www.johncurtinhotel.com; 29 Lygon St, Carlton; 🚃1, 3, 8, 64, 72)

La Mama
THEATRE

16 ⭐ Map p114, F4

La Mama is historically significant in Melbourne's theatre scene. This tiny, intimate forum produces new Australian works and experimental theatre, and has a reputation for developing emerging playwrights. It's a ramshackle building with an open-air bar. Shows also run at its larger **Courthouse Theater** at 349 Drummond St, so check tickets carefully for the correct location. (📞03-9347 6948; www.lamama.com.au; 205 Faraday St, Carlton; 🚊1, 8)

Imax
CINEMA

17 ⭐ Map p114, G5

Animal and adventure films in 3D screen on a grand scale here, with movies specially made for these giant screens. (📞03-9663 5454; www.imaxmelbourne.com.au; Melbourne Museum, Rathdowne St, Carlton; 🚌Tourist Shuttle, 🚌86, 96)

Shopping

Lab Perfumery
BEAUTY

18 🔒 Map p114, G2

Feeling right at home along this boutique stretch of Rathdowne St, the Lab has an interesting range of organic, Australian-made skincare products, fragrances and beauty kits. Products for men, too. (www.thelabperfumery.com.au; 360 Rathdowne St, North Carlton; ⊙10am-5pm Sun-Tue, to 6pm Wed-Sat; 🚊1, 8)

La Parisienne
FOOD

19 🔒 Map p114, F4

A French interloper in this most Italian of streets, Parisienne specialises in small goods and take-home dishes that are authentically Gallic. *Boudin blanc* and *noir* (white and dark pork

sausage), duck *confit* and its famous pâtés and terrines will not disappoint. It also does a nice range of bread and little pies that are perfect for picnic provisions, and keeps a range of evocatively packaged pantry items. (📞03-9349 1852; 290 Lygon St, Carlton; ⊙9am-6.30pm Mon-Sat, from 10am Sun; 🚊1, 8, 16)

Readings
BOOKS

20 🔒 Map p114, F3

A potter around this defiantly prospering indie bookshop can occupy an entire afternoon if you're so inclined. There's a dangerously loaded (and good-value) specials table, switched-on staff and everyone from Lacan to *Charlie & Lola* on the shelves. Its exterior 'housemate wanted' board is legendary. Also in St Kilda and the city centre. (www.readings.com.au; 309 Lygon St, Carlton; ⊙8am-11pm Mon-Fri, 9am-11pm Sat, 9am-9pm Sun; 🚌Tourist Shuttle, 🚊1, 8)

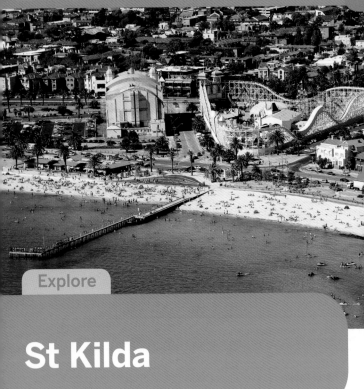

Explore

St Kilda

It's not just the palm trees, bay vistas, briny breezes and pink sunsets that give St Kilda its appeal. It's the eclectic cast of characters – junkies to yuppies, musos to backpackers and beautiful people to winos – all united by a wonderful sense of community. Throw in historical pubs, live music, chic restaurants, Eastern European cake stores and a rickety 1920s roller-coaster and you've got St Kilda.

The Sights in a Day

Start in East St Kilda along Carlisle St to soak up its Eastern European heritage, with fresh bagels at **Glick's** (p129) and a visit to the **Jewish Museum of Australia** (p127) to put the area into context. Then head along Acland St, one of St Kilda's most lively, for a morning tea of *kugelhopf* (marble cake) at the iconic **Monarch Cake Shop** (p128).

If the sun's out spend the afternoon lazing on St Kilda Beach, and perhaps get out on the water with kitesurfing at **Kite Republic** (p128), or a **stand-up paddleboarding** (p127) tour to visit penguins. For a drink at sunset head to the **Esplanade Hotel** (p133) or **Republica** (p131), directly on the beach.

As soon as the sun goes down, St Kilda steps up a gear as revellers descend from all over Melbourne for a debaucherous night out. Grab a seafood dinner at **Claypots** (p129), and then be spoiled for choice of craft beer at the **Local Taphouse** (p131). Run the gauntlet along seedy Fitzroy St back to the Espy for live bands from a choice of three stages. Finish up at the **Vineyard** (p131), a bar well known for its love of partying.

 Top Sights

St Kilda Foreshore (p124)

Best of St Melbourne

Drinking
Local Taphouse (p131)

George Lane Bar (p131)

Eating
Attica (p141)

Lau's Family Kitchen (p128)

Monarch Cake Shop (p128)

Getting There

🚋 **Tram** 3, 16, 67, 86, 96, 112

Top Sights
St Kilda Foreshore

While there are palm-fringed promenades, a parkland strand and a long stretch of sand, St Kilda's seaside appeal is more Brighton, England, than *Baywatch,* despite 20-odd years of glitzy development. The esplanade that runs along the waterfront takes you past the beach, historical buildings and grassy embankments perfect for lazing about with a picnic. The area is in constant flux with risk of developers marching in to turn it into high-rises, but for now remains safe.

👁 Map p126, A3

Jacka Blvd

🚊 16, 96

St Kilda Beach

Don't Miss

Historic Landmarks

St Kilda Pier is a much-loved icon that's great for a stroll. At its end sits the quaint **pavilion kiosk**, which burned down in 2003 (a year short of its centenary) and was faithfully restored in 2006. Other striking architecture along the promenade includes the heritage-listed **Palais Theatre** (☎03-9525 3240, tickets 13 61 00; www.palaistheatre.net.au; Lower Esplanade; ☐3a, 16, 79, 96) from around 1927, the grand **Esplanade Hotel** (p133) from around 1878 and the Moorish-style **St Kilda Sea Baths** (c 1910).

Luna Park

Opened in 1912, **Luna Park** (☎03-9525 5033; www.lunapark.com.au; 18 Lower Esplanade; single ride adult/child $11/9, unlimited rides $48/38; ☐16, 96) retains the feel of an old-style amusement park, with creepy Mr Moon's gaping mouth swallowing you up as you enter. The heritage-listed 'Scenic Railway' is the oldest operating roller-coaster in the world. There's a beautifully baroque carousel with hand-painted horses, swans and chariots, and the full complement of gut-churning rides.

St Kilda Beach

Tourists may not flock to Melbourne for its city beaches, but come hot weather St Kilda's the place to be. Cool off with a swim in the bay, kiteboarding (all the rage November to April), stand-up paddleboarding (SUP) or windsurfing.

Penguins

The breakwater near St Kilda Pier is home to a colony of little penguins that have, incredibly, chosen the city's most crowded suburb in which to reside. During summer you can visit and learn about them on an eco-themed stand-up paddle-boarding tour (p127).

☑ **Top Tips**

► The weekly **Esplanade Market** (www.esplanademarket.com; btwn Cavell & Fitzroy Sts; ☉10am-5pm Sun; ☐96) has a kilometre of trestle tables joined end-to-end with individually crafted products from toys to organic soaps and metal sculptures.

► In December, the St Kilda Open-Air Cinema screens cult classics by the seaside. You can rent blankets, deckchairs ($4) and bean-bag lounges ($7).

► Neighbouring Elwood Beach is a less busy and touristy alternative to St Kilda.

✗ **Take a Break**

Catch the ocean breeze over coffee and cake and enjoy unhindered bay and city views from historic **St Kilda Pier kiosk**. Grab breakfast or a sunset beer at Republica (p131), St Kilda's closest thing to a beach bar.

400 m
0.25 miles

ST KILDA WEST

ST KILDA

ELWOOD

St Kilda Foreshore

Port Phillip

Hobsons Bay

Albert Park

Peanut Farm Reserve

Luna Park

O'Donnell Gardens

Alfred Square

St Kilda Botanical Gardens

Catani Gardens

St Kilda Pier

Linden Arts Centre & Gallery

St Kilda Sea Baths

Kite Republic

Sunset Eco Penguin Tours

Chapel St

St Kilda Rd

Brighton Rd

Marine Pde

Jacka Blvd

Barkly St

Acland St

Carlisle St

Inkerman St

Alma Rd

Grey St

Fitzroy St

Beaconsfield Pde

Canterbury Rd

Sights

Jewish Museum of Australia

MUSEUM

1 ◉ Map p126, D1

Interactive displays tell the history of Australia's Jewish community from the earliest days of European settlement, while permanent exhibitions celebrate Judaism's rich cycle of festivals and holy days. The museum also has a good curatorial reputation for its contemporary art exhibitions. By car, follow St Kilda Rd from St Kilda Junction, then turn left at Alma Rd. (📞03-9834 3600; www. jewishmuseum.com.au; 26 Alma Rd, St Kilda; adult/child/family $10/5/20; ⏱10am-4pm Tue-Thu, to 5pm Sun, closed Jewish holy days; 🚋3, 67)

St Kilda Botanical Gardens

GARDENS

2 ◉ Map p126, D4

Taking pride of place on the southern line of the Barkly, Carlisle and Blessington St triangle, the botanic gardens are an unexpected haven from the St Kilda hustle. Wide gravel paths invite a leisurely stroll, and there are plenty of shady spots to sprawl on the open lawns. There are local indigenous plants and a subtropical rainforest conservatory to ponder. (📞03-9209 6777; www.portphillip.vic.gov.au; cnr Blessington & Tennyson Sts, St Kilda; ⏱sunrise-sunset; 🚋96)

CHRISTOPHER GROENHOUT / GETTY IMAGES ©

St Kilda Pier (p125)

Sunset Eco Penguin Tour

ECOTOUR

3 ◉ Map p126, A2

See St Kilda's penguin colony from around October to April (minimum two people), while you navigate your stand-up paddleboard. (📞0416 184 994; www. supb.com.au; 2hr penguin tours $130; 🚋96)

Linden Arts Centre & Gallery

GALLERY

4 ◉ Map p126, B3

Housed in a wrought-iron-clad 1870s mansion, Linden champions the work of emerging artists. The annual post-card show, which coincides with the St Kilda Festival in February/March,

Local Life

Beer & Bowls

St Kilda Bowling Club (Map p126, B1; www.stkildasportsclub.com.au; 66 Fitzroy St, St Kilda; noon-11pm Sun-Thu, to 1am Fri & Sat; 16, 96, 112) is a popular local hang-out where the only dress code is 'shoes off'. It's a fabulously intact old clubhouse tucked behind a neatly trimmed hedge and a splendid bowling green. The bar serves drinks at 'club prices' (ie cheap) and you'll be joined by St Kilda's hippest on Sunday afternoons. Kick off your shoes, roll a few bowls, knock back beers and watch the sun go down (along with your bowling accuracy).

is a highlight. (03-9534 0099; www. lindenarts.org; 26 Acland St, St Kilda; 1-5pm Tue-Fri, 11am-5pm Sat & Sun; 16, 96)

Kite Republic

KITEBOARDING

5 Map p126, A3

Offers kiteboarding lessons, tours and equipment; also a good source of info. In winter it can arrange snow-kiting at Mt Hotham. Also rents SUPs and Street SUPs. (03-9537 0644; www.kiterepublic. com.au; St Kilda Seabaths, 4/10-18 Jacka Blvd, St Kilda; 1hr lessons $90; 10am-7pm)

Aurora Spa Retreat

DAY SPA

There's a creative menu of wellness treatments ranging from water-based massage and full-body wraps to three- and four-hour retreat packages, all within a beautiful chic setting at the

Prince hotel (see 22 Map p126, B2). Good deals can be had midweek. (03-9536 1130; www.aurorasparetreat.com; 2 Acland St, St Kilda; 1hr from $120; 8.30am-8pm Mon-Fri, to 6pm Sat, 10am-7pm Sun; 3a, 16, 96, 112)

Eating

Lau's Family Kitchen

CHINESE $$

6 Map p126, B2

The owner's family comes with absolutely flawless pedigree (father Gilbert Lau is the former owner of famed Flower Drum) and the restaurant is in a lovely leafy location. The mainly Cantonese menu is simple, and dishes are beautifully done, with a few surprises thrown in for more adventurous diners. Make a reservation for one of the two dinner sittings. (03-8598 9880; www. lauskitchen.com.au; 4 Acland St, St Kilda; mains $25-38; dinner sittings 6pm & 8pm; 16, 96)

Monarch Cake Shop

DESSERTS, EUROPEAN $

7 Map p126, C4

St Kilda's Eastern European cake shops have long drawn crowds that come to peer at the sweetly stocked windows. Monarch is a favourite – its *kugelhopf* (marble cake), plum cake and poppy-seed cheesecake can't be beaten. In business since 1934, not much has changed here with its wonderful buttery aromas and old-time atmosphere. Also does good coffee. (03-9534 2972; www.monarchcakes.com.au; 103 Acland St, St Kilda; slice of cake $5; 8am-10pm; 96)

Monk Bodhi Dharma
CAFE $$

 8 Map p126, E4

Monk Bodhi Dharma's hidden location, down an alley off Carlisle St (next to Safeway), means it doesn't get much passing foot traffic, which is lucky given that this cosy brick cafe has enough devotees as it is. A former 1920s bakehouse, these days it's all about transcendental vegetarian food, house-ade Bircher muesli and house-roasted single-estate coffee. Book ahead for Friday night dinners. (03-9534 7250; www.monkbodhidharma.com; Rear, 202 Carlisle St, Balaclava; breakfast $8.50-18.50; 7am-5pm Mon-Fri, 8am-5pm Sat & Sun; 3, 16, 79)

Cicciolina
MEDITERRANEAN $$

9 Map p126, C4

This warm room of dark wood, subdued lighting and pencil sketches is a St Kilda institution. The inspired Modern Australian/Mediterranean menu is smart and generous, and the service warm. You can only make bookings for lunch; for dinner, eat early or while away your wait in the moody little back bar. (www.cicciolina-stkilda.com.au; 130 Acland St, St Kilda; mains $17-43; noon-10pm; 16, 96)

Claypots
SEAFOOD $$

10 Map p126, C4

A local favourite, Claypots serves up seafood in its namesake dish. Get in early to both get a seat and ensure the good stuff is still available, as hot items go fast. It also has a spot at the South Melbourne Market (p62). (03-9534 1282; 213 Barkly St, St Kilda; mains $25-35; noon-3pm & 6pm-1am; 96)

Si Señor
MEXICAN $

11 Map p126, E4

One of the latest additions to Melbourne's Mexican restaurant takeover, Si Señor is one of the most authentic. Tasty spit-and-grilled meats are heaped onto soft corn tortillas under direction of its Mexican owner. If you've overdone the hot sauce, cool it down with an authentic *horchata,* a delicious rice-milk and cinnamon drink. (www.sisenor.net.au; 193 Carlisle St, Balaclava; tacos $5-7, tortas $13-15; 11.30pm-late; ; 3, 16, 79)

Newmarket Hotel
LATIN AMERICAN $$

12 Map p126, D2

In typical St Kilda fashion, this historic pub has received a cosmetic enhancement, though thankfully it's been done

 Local Life

Glick's Bagels

No-frills **Glick's** (www.glicks.com.au; 33a Carlisle St, Balaclava; bagels $4-10; 5.30am-8pm Mon-Fri & Sun, 7.30pm-midnight Sat; 3, 16, 79) bakery keeps the local Jewish community happy with bagels baked and boiled in-house; kosher options are available. Stick with the classics and try the 'New Yorker' with cream cheese and egg salad.

REBECCA SKINNER / GETTY IMAGES ©

Lentil as Anything

tastefully courtesy of a modern refurb by renowned Six Degrees architects. The menu's Latin American–inspired, so expect Mexican street food, wood-barbecued meats and premium steaks. Lunch specials are excellent value, and there's a top-shelf bar, too. (☏03-9537 1777; www.newmarketstkilda.com.au; 34 Inkerman St, St Kilda; meals from $15; ☺noon-3pm & 6-10.30pm; ☐3, 67)

Mirka's at Tolarno
INTERNATIONAL, ITALIAN $$

13 Map p126, B1

Beloved artist Mirka Mora's murals grace the walls in this dining room with a history (it's been delighting diners since the early '60s), part of Tolarno Hotel. Guy Grossi's Italian menu has some rustic classics, like veal saltimbocca, mixed with interesting surprises such as walnut and pear gnocchi with gorgonzola. There's also a four-course sharing menu ($60). (☏03-9525 3088; www.mirkatolarnohotel.com; Tolarno Hotel, 42 Fitzroy St, St Kilda; mains $26-32; ☺6pm-late; ☐16, 96, 112)

Lentil as Anything
VEGETARIAN $

14 Map p126, C4

Choosing from the organic, vegetarian menu is easy. Deciding what to pay can be hard. This unique not-for-profit operation provides training and educational opportunities for marginalised people, as well as tasty vegetarian food. Whatever you end up paying for your meal goes towards helping new migrants, refugees, people with disabilities and the long-term unemployed. Also at the Abbotsford Convent (p106). (www.lentilasanything.com; 41 Blessington St, St Kilda; by donation; ☺11am-9pm; ☑; ☐16, 96)

Mr Wolf
PIZZA $$

15 Map p126, C3

Local celeb chef Karen Martini's casual but stylish space is renowned for its crisp Roma-style pizzas. There's also a great menu of antipasti and pastas that display her flair for matching ingredients. (☏03-9534 0255; www.mrwolf.com.au; 9-15 Inkerman St, St Kilda; pizzas $20-25; ☺5pm-late Tue-Sun, from noon Fri-Sun; ☐16)

Drinking

Local Taphouse BAR

16 Map p126, E3

Reminiscent of an old-school Brooklyn bar. Prop up to its dark-wood polished bar and scratch your head while deciding what to order from the 19 craft beers on tap or the impressive bottle list to order. There's a beer garden upstairs, while downstairs has chesterfield couches, an open fire and indoor bocce pit. It's also known for its live comedy nights. (www.thelocal.com.au; 184 Carlisle St, St Kilda; ⏱noon-late; 🚊16, 78, 🚉Balaclava)

George Lane Bar BAR

17 🚌 Map p126, B1

Hidden behind the hulk of the George Hotel, tucked away off Grey St, this little bar is a good rabbit hole to dive into. Its pleasantly ad-hoc decor is a relief from the inch-of-its-life design aesthetic elsewhere. There are DJs (and queues) on the weekends. (www.georgelanebar.com.au; 1 George Lane, St Kilda; ⏱7pm-1am Thu-Sun; 🚊96, 16)

Republica BAR

18 🚌 Map p126, A3

Opening right up to St Kilda Beach, Republica is the closest you'll get to a beach bar in Melbourne. A great spot for a sunset beer or cocktail lounging in a hanging wicker chair, but you can also start the day here by the sea with breakfast and coffee. (www.republica.net.au; 10-18 Jacka Blvd, St Kilda Sea Baths, St Kilda; ⏱11.30am-1am Mon-Fri, 9am-1am Sat & Sun; 🛜; 🚊3a, 16, 96)

St Kilda Dispensary CAFE

19 Map p126, D4

In what was once the first dispensary in the southern hemisphere during the 1940s, this cafe keeps with the medical theme with tiled counters, test tubes and beakers and a menu that prescribes the good stuff: organic coffees, breakfast rolls and tuna melts. Cash only. (13 Brighton Rd, St Kilda; ⏱7am-4pm Mon-Fri, 8am-4pm Sat & Sun; 🚊16, 67, 79)

Vineyard BAR

20 Map p126, C4

An old favourite, the Vineyard has the perfect corner position and a courtyard BBQ that attracts crowds of backpackers and scantily clad young locals who enjoy themselves so

 Local Life

Carlisle Wine Bar

Locals love the often-rowdy, wine-worshipping former butcher's shop of the **Carlisle Wine Bar** (Map p126, E4; 📞03-9531 3222; www.carlislewinebar.com.au; 137 Carlisle St, Balaclava; ⏱3pm-1am Mon-Fri, 11am-1am Sat & Sun; 🚊3, 16, 🚉Balaclava). The staff will treat you like a regular and find you a glass of something special, or effortlessly throw together a cocktail amid the weekend rush. The rustic Italian food is good, too. Carlisle St runs east off St Kilda Rd.

Understand

Melbourne's Live-Music Scene

Melbourne's cultural image has involved music since producing two of the most enduringly fascinating talents of the 19th and early 20th centuries. Opera diva Dame Nellie Melba was an international star who lived overseas for many years but retained a sentimental attachment to her home town (hence the name). Percy Grainger, whose innovative compositions and performances prefigured many forms of 20th-century music, was born and brought up in Melbourne. Grainger's eccentric genius extended beyond music to the design of clothing and objects; he was also known for his transgressive sex life. His life story is on display at the Grainger Museum in Parkville.

More recently, Melbourne's live-music scene exploded in the mid-1960s with a band called the Loved Ones, who broke the imitative mould of American '50s rock 'n' roll. The early 1970s saw groups such as AC/DC, Skyhooks and Daddy Cool capture the experience of ordinary Melbourne life in their lyrics for the first time. By the end of that decade, punk had descended. Nick Cave's Boys Next Door and the so-called 'Little Bands' shrieked their way through gigs at St Kilda's Crystal Ballroom (now the George Hotel). Bands and performers that grew out of (and beyond) this scene included the Birthday Party (evolving into Nick Cave and the Bad Seeds), the Models, Dead Can Dance, X, Primitive Calculators and the Moodists.

The '80s pub-rock scene also gave birth to Crowded House, Paul Kelly, Hunters & Collectors and Australian Crawl, while the '90s and 2000s punk/grunge era saw the likes of the Cosmic Psychos, the Meanies, Powder Monkeys, Magic Dirt and Eddy Current Suppression Ring carry the torch passed on from their late-'70s predecessors.

Despite the ongoing threat of music venues being closed down due to noise complaints by some inner-city residents, Melbourne still has a plethora of great venues spread throughout the city and inner suburbs and remains the live-music capital of Australia. Melbourne draws musicians from around the country. The current buzz bands include the Drones, the Twerps, UV Race and King Gizzard & the Lizard Wizard.

much they drown out the neighbouring roller-coaster. Sunday-afternoon sessions are big here. (www.thevineyard.com.au; 71a Acland St, St Kilda; ⏱10.30am-3.30am Mon-Fri, 10am-3.30am Sat & Sun; 🚊3a, 16, 96)

Entertainment

Esplanade Hotel
LIVE MUSIC

21 ⭐ Map p126, A2

Rock-pigs rejoice. The Espy remains gloriously shabby and welcoming to all. A mix of local and international bands play nightly, everything from rock 'n' roll to hip hop either in the legendary Gershwin Room, the front bar or down in the basement. (The Espy; ☎03-9534 0211; www.espy.com.au; 11 The Esplanade, St Kilda; ⏱noon-1am Sun-Wed, to 3am Thu-Sat; 🚊16, 96)

Prince Bandroom
LIVE MUSIC

22 ⭐ Map p126, B2

The Prince is a much-loved St Kilda venue, with quality international and local rock, indie, DJs and hip hop bands having graced its stage. Its leafy balcony and raucous downstairs bar are added attractions. These days it leans more towards dance and electropop acts. (☎03-9536 1168; www.

⬤ Local Life
Pure Pop Records
A well-loved record store, **Pure Pop Records** (Map p126, C4; www.purepop.com.au; 221 Barkly St, St Kilda; ⏱10am-6pm Mon-Wed, to 11pm Thu-Sun; 🚊96) stocks mainly independent releases and a great selection of local music. It also doubles as one of the most intimate live-music spaces in Melbourne; gigs are rarely advertised and, therefore, rather special. Past acts have included secret gigs by the White Stripes and Lee Ranaldo.

princebandroom.com.au; 29 Fitzroy St, St Kilda; 🚊16, 96, 112)

Shopping

Bookhouse
BOOKS

23 🔒 Map p126, C2

A much-loved local, Bookhouse recently relocated from Fitzroy St to this quiet backstreet shop, where you might find a quality copy of a Chomsky, Kerouac or beautiful coffee-table book on the shelves, as well as a great selection of Australiana and Melbourne-specific titles. (www.bookhousestkilda.com.au; 52 Robe St, St Kilda; ⏱10am-6pm Wed-Sun; 🚊3, 67)

The Best of
Melbourne

Melbourne's Best Walks

Melbourne's Best...

Melbourne at dusk
ANDREW PEACOCK / GETTY IMAGES ©

Best Walks
A Seaside St Kilda Stroll

🏃 The Walk

With its palm-fringed promenades and long stretch of sand, St Kilda is made for wandering. It was once a playground full of dance halls, a fun park, theatres, sea baths and gardens. Despite a roller-coaster history of seediness and the more recent glitzy development, there are still remnants of the art deco mansions, and more than an air of the decadent heyday. This walk takes you through some of this seaside vibe.

Start St Kilda Pier; 🚊16, 96

Finish St Kilda Botanical Gardens; 🚊96

Length 3km; two hours

🍴 Take a Break

There's no better setting for coffee and cake than in the historic St Kilda Pier kiosk. You'll find plenty of cafes and restaurants along Acland St, but we recommend bypassing them until you hit Barkly St where you can feast on seafood at Claypots (p129).

Palais Theatre

RICHARD NEBESKY / GETTY IMAGES ©

❶ St Kilda Pier & Kiosk

Stroll along historic **St Kilda Pier** (p125) for panoramic city and Port Phillip Bay views. The kiosk burnt down in 2003, just a year shy of its centenary, but was restored in 2006.

❷ St Kilda Beach

Keep walking onto famous **St Kilda Beach** (p125). When summer hits, it packs out with locals and tourists looking for a patch of sand. While it may not be azure waters and white sands, for a city beach it's a winner.

❸ Linden Arts Centre & Gallery

Dust off the sand and head to the quiet end of Acland St to find **Linden Arts Centre & Gallery** (p127). The not-for-profit gallery is housed in a historical Victorian mansion and showcases contemporary works.

❹ Esplanade Hotel

Continue down Acland St and onto the Esplanade for one of the city's most iconic rock pubs.

Opened in 1878, the crumbling mansion of **'the Espy (p133)'** is one of Australia's longest continuously running live-music venues. Enjoy beer with foreshore views on its terrace.

❺ Palais Theatre

Further along the Esplanade, the **Palais Theatre** (p125) is one of the best examples of art deco in Melbourne. This former cinema has acted as a concert venue for many years hosting ballet, opera, and local and international bands.

❻ Luna Park

Across the road you'll hear the screams from people hurtling on the historic roller-coaster at **Luna Park** (p125). Mr Moon has been swallowing people at the entrance since it opened in 1912. There's the usual whiplash-inducing rides and a beautiful baroque carousel.

❼ Monarch Cake Shop

In business since 1934, the **Monarch** (p128) is one of the best Eastern European cake stores on the strip and is known for delicious *kugelhopf* (marble cake).

❽ St Kilda Botanical Gardens

Escape the hustle in the backstreets off Acland St, where the **St Kilda Botanical Gardens** (p127) remain a local favourite. Spread out a picnic blanket among indigenous plants and trees.

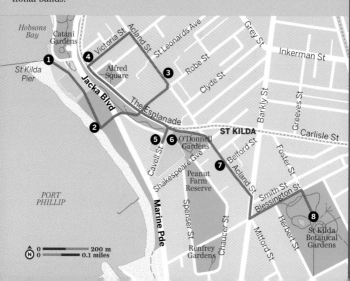

Best Walks
Classic City Melbourne

🏃 The Walk

If at first glance Melbourne seems thin on genuine world-class sights, your outlook will be swayed by a morning or afternoon absorbing the city's unique offerings. Melbourne has something for everyone's taste, from the grandeur of gold-rush-era buildings to green spaces, art galleries to graffiti-filled laneways, hip bars and trendy restaurants to markets and history.

Start Flinders Street Station; 🚃Flinders St

Finish Queen Victoria Market; 🚋9, 55, 57, 59

Length 3km; four hours

✕ Take a Break

For the quintessential Melbourne laneway dining experience, you can't beat tasty Spanish tapas at oh-so-cool MoVida (p38). For a more classic setting, duck into Young & Jackson's (p37) for coffee and cake, an upscale pub meal or a cold beer.

❶ Federation Square

While its quirky design may have critics, **Fed Square** (p24) has become accepted as the city's gathering point. It's also home to the world-class Ian Potter Centre: NGV Australia art gallery and ACMI.

❷ Birrarung Marr

An oasis in the heart of the city, **Birrarung Marr** (p26) offers a peaceful stroll alongside the Yarra River through indigenous vegetation, and Aboriginal installations and sculptures. It's a scenic place for a BBQ by the river, and provides fantastic photo ops.

❸ Hosier Lane

In a city famed for street art, **Hosier Lane** (p34) is ground zero, attracting everyone from graffiti artists to curious photo-snapping locals and tourists. Expect graffiti, stencils, murals and paste-ups.

❹ Old Treasury Building

Wind your way up Flinders Lane and Collins St to this stately 19th-

Chinatown

TOM COCKREM / GETTY IMAGES ©

century Renaissance Revival–style **building** (p35). Today a museum, its grandeur is symbolic of the wealth of the gold-rush boom years in the 1850s. Further along Spring St is majestic Parliament House.

❺ Chinatown

This strip of Chinese (and other Asian) restaurants is a legacy from the influx of Chinese gold-rush settlers in the 1850s. Put it into context by visiting the **Chinese Museum** (p34).

❻ State Library of Victoria

Duck into this stunning **library** (p34) to learn why Melbourne is recognised by Unesco as a City of Literature. It houses more than two million books, a stunning reading room, fantastic exhibits and Ned Kelly's armour.

❼ Old Melbourne Gaol

It may have closed its doors in 1929, but this formidable bluestone **prison** (p35) remains as grim as ever. It's one of Melbourne's most popular museums.

Tour the cells and learn about executions of notorious inmates such as Ned Kelly.

❽ Queen Victoria Market

One of Melbourne's most famous land-

marks, this 19th-century **market** (p28) is a great place to buy fresh produce, gourmet foods and Australiana souvenirs.

Best
Eating

Melburnians love their food. The city has a multicultural culinary scene that has few peers around the world. Throw in a highly developed cafe culture, growing street-food and food-truck scene, and all manner of designer dens where serious eating is the order of the day and you have a true culinary capital.

GREG ELMS / GETTY IMAGES ©

Fine Dining to Pub Grub

At the top of the city's food chain, fine dining thrives. You'll find menus that rove across regions and riff on influences. Pub grub is also a big part of the city's eating-out repertoire, and ranges from upmarket gastropub restaurants to basic counter-meal service.

Dishing Up Diversity

Take 140 cultures, mix and let simmer for a few decades. While the recipe might not be quite that simple, Victoria's culinary habits are truly multi-cultural. Many Melburnians have grown up with at least one other culinary heritage besides the rather grim Anglo-Australian fare of the mid-20th century, and they are also inveterate travellers. This makes for a city of adventurous palates.

Food Trucks

Melbourne has long had an association with food vans; a game of suburban footy isn't complete without greasy vans dishing out meat pies and hot chips to fans. But getting quality food from a van is a different matter. Taking the cue from LA, food trucks have begun plying the streets of Melbourne in recent years, from where you can get anything from tacos and burgers to BBQ meats and croco-dile pies.

Best Splurge

Vue de Monde Melbourne's preferred spot for occasion dining with views to match its name. (p37)

Flower Drum The city's most celebrated Chinese restaurant with sumptuous Cantonese food. (p39)

WoodLand House Experience memorable tasting menus in a Victorian terrace house. (p74)

MoVida Gorge on tasty Spanish tapas in a street-art covered laneway setting. (p38)

Lau's Family Kitchen Modern Asian in a chic St Kilda eatery. (p128)

Best Local & Indigenous Cuisine

Charcoal Lane Try a kangaroo burger, wallaby tartare or native flora. (p99)

Vue de Monde Local ingredients such as Flinders Island lamb fused with classic French dishes. (p37)

Best Cheap Eats

Camy Shanghai Dumpling Down a plastic plate full of dumplings with BYO beer at this student-filled institution. (p40)

Thy Thy 1 One of Richmond's best-known cheap and cheerful Vietnamese places. (p86)

Huxtaburger Glazed brioche burgers for under a tenner. (p99)

Minh Minh Red-hot Laotian dishes on Victoria St. (p86)

Andrew's Burgers Classic juicy burgers and chips at a steal. (p64)

Best Food Cafes

Cumulus Inc Breakfast on smoked ocean trout or house-made crumpets at one of the city's best early-morning spots. (p38)

St Ali Feast on corn fritters and haloumi in this award-winning cafe. (p63)

Mart 130 Great breakfasts and light lunches in a converted tram stop. (p64)

Best Authentic Cuisine

DOC Espresso Home-made pastas, pizza and excellent Negronis. (p117)

Demitri's Feast Tasty Greek dishes at a popular weekend spot. (p85)

Abla's Indulge in a gut-busting authentic Lebanese banquet. (p118)

Tiamo Classic Italian cafe fare at this Lygon St favourite. (p118)

Rumi Excellent authentic Middle Eastern dishes. (p91)

Colonel Tans Thai chefs whip up curries and betel leaf snacks. (p74)

Best Seafood

Rockpool Bar & Grill Neil Perry serves up his signature seafood bar. (p53)

Albert Park Hotel Oyster Bar & Grill Throw back oysters and wood-barbecued fish. (p63)

Worth a Trip

Award-winning restaurant **Attica** (☏ 03-9530 0111; www.attica.com.au; 74 Glen Eira Rd, Ripponlea; 8-course tasting menu $190; ⏱ 6.30pm-late Wed-Sat; 🚃 67, 🚉 Ripponlea) serves Ben Shewry's creative dishes degustation-style. Staff perform minor miracles on cue with a sprinkle of this or a drop of that to finish each dish. Book several months in advance. Follow Brighton Rd south to Glen Eira Rd.

Best
Parks & Gardens

If Victoria is the garden state, then Melbourne is the garden city. You'll enjoy an abundance of green spaces dotted around town. Whether you're checking out native species in the botanical gardens, admiring 19th-century heritage gardens or picnicking like a local in inner-city green spaces, you'll never be short of a leafy refuge.

TOM COCKREM / GETTY IMAGES ©

Best Inner-City Green Space

Birrarung Marr Wander through the grassy knolls, river promenades and thoughtful planting of indigenous flora at this city park area. (p26)

Flagstaff Gardens See possums and a variety of trees from Moreton Bay figs to eucalypts, some more than 100 years old. (p37)

Fitzroy Gardens On the fringe of the central business district (CBD), you'll find sprawling lawns and grand avenues; also home to Cook's Cottage. (p85)

Herring Island Park On an island in the middle of the Yarra you can see the original trees and grasses of the Yarra. (p73)

Best Botanical Gardens

Royal Botanic Gardens Up there with the best botanical gardens in the world, with herb gardens and an indigenous rainforest. (p68)

St Kilda Botanical Gardens A hidden gem in St Kilda's quiet backstreets, where you can laze around with a good book like a local. (p127)

Best
With Kids

GLENN BEANLAND / GETTY IMAGES ©

Best Parks & Gardens

Birrarung Marr Within this green space, ArtPlay runs fun creative workshops. (p26)

Ian Potter Foundation Children's Garden Interactive garden where kids can discover the natural world. (p69)

Fitzroy Gardens Explore Cook's Cottage and the Fairies Tree. (p85)

Best Museums

Melbourne Museum Natural and cultural delights for kids of all ages. (p110)

Scienceworks Fun and interactive science and sports exhibits, plus a planetarium. (p57)

Old Melbourne Gaol Educational and memorable for kids over 10 who can explore the historic jail cells. (p35)

National Sports Museum Test your footy, cricket and netball skills after being inspired by the legends of Australian sport. (p83)

Best Outdoors

St Kilda Foreshore Build sandcastles and splash in the bay on summer days. (p124)

Luna Park With bumper cars and roller-coasters, this amusement park guarantees fun. (p125)

Best Animal Encounters

Sea Life Melbourne Aquarium Watch sharks cruise around and spot penguins on ice. (p35)

Collingwood Children's Farm Inner-city farm with loads of frolicking animals. (p107)

Royal Melbourne Zoo Australia's oldest zoo with a large number of native animals. (p116)

Best Rainy-Day Activities

ACMI Kids can watch films and play video games. (p25)

State Library of Victoria Check out Ned Kelly's armour. (p34)

IMAX Enthralling 3-D movies. (p121)

Best
Drinking

Melbourne's bars are legendary, from laneway hideaways to brassy corner establishments. The same goes for coffee, which is a local obsession as consumers, roasters and baristas strive for the perfect cup. Out of the city, shopping strips are embedded with shopfront drinking holes: try Fitzroy, Collingwood, Prahran and St Kilda, which, despite rapid gentrification, still retain plenty of character-filled oldies.

Craft Beer & Breweries

Until recently, thirsty Melburnians were given the choice of two or three mainstream beers on tap (and perhaps an interstate lager if one was feeling adventurous). But in the last few years things have changed with the emergence of microbreweries and craft-beer bars to meet the demands of beer aficionados and those who've started to treat their drinking more seriously.

Celebrated Coffee

Melbourne's coffee tradition stems back to the arrival of Italian immigrants, but these days it's not just a shot of strong espresso on the menu. Direct-trade single origin beans and speciality brews such as siphon, pour over and cold drip are on the rise. There's a reason Melbourne's coffee is so celebrated: much of it is roasted here.

LONELY PLANET / GETTY IMAGES ©

Best Rooftop Bars

Naked for Satan Watch the sun go down over Fitzroy. (p100)

Madame Brussels Indulge in a jug of housemade Pimms amid Astroturf and polo shirts. (p41)

Rooftop Cinema Perch high above the city at the top of Curtain House. (p43)

Lui Bar At the top of the Rialto building, this classy cocktail bar takes the standard to dizzying heights. (p41)

Corner Hotel Richmond's old-school band venue has a rooftop bar attracting a mixed and lively crowd. (p87)

Best Laneway Bars

Bar Americano Standing-room only at this superb city cocktail bar. (p41)

Cherry Legendary divey rock bar tucked down ACDC Lane. (p31)

Chuckle Park Order a cocktail jug from the parked caravan. (p41)

Croft Institute It's a science in itself just finding this lab-themed bar. (p42)

George Lane Bar Tucked away behind St Kilda's George Hotel. (p131)

Best Beer Gardens

Windsor Castle Hotel Tiki-themed garden in Windsor's backstreets. (p76)

Boatbuilders Yard Beer and bocce riverside. (p54)

Retreat Popular Brunswick local with backyard vibe. (p91)

Ponyfish Island Technically not a garden but one of the best outdoor bars; perched in the middle of the Yarra. (p53)

Best Coffee

Market Lane Try an on-site roasted coffee as you peruse the Prahran Market. (p76)

Seven Seeds Out-of-the-way warehouse cafe with superb coffee. (p119)

Auction Rooms House-roasted single-origin beans; some of the best coffee in the city. (p119)

Industry Beans Try some cafe latte pearls at this coffee chemistry cafe. (p102)

Best Rock Pubs & Bars

Esplanade Hotel A St Kilda classic; the Espy's front bar has live bands for free, where you can drink with the locals. (p133)

Tote Grungy Collingwood local with excellent bands and the best jukebox in town. (p102)

Yellow Bird Owned by a local musician; knock back drinks to a great soundtrack. (p75)

Cherry Iconic city laneway rock bar. (p31)

Best for Beer Snobs

Mountain Goat Brewery Urban Richmond brewer with tasting paddles. (p87)

Local Taphouse One of St Kilda's finest establishments for craft beer. (p131)

Alehouse Project Beer-hall-style seating and great craft-beer selection. (p91)

Best Cocktails

Lui Bar Try the signature macadamia martini and gaze out over the city. (p41)

Bar Americano Expertly made classic cocktails. (p41)

Everleigh Sophisticated 'golden era' cocktails in a hidden upstairs Fitzroy bar. (p100)

Panama Dining Room Leafy Collingwood views with serious cocktails to match. (p100)

Best
For Free

ANDREW WATSON / GETTY IMAGES ©

Melbourne may be at the higher end of the price scale but there is a decent picking of free offerings in the city. Whether it's gallery-hopping or checking out street art and museums, there are plenty of ways to save those pennies.

Best Museums & Art

Ian Potter Centre: NGV Australia Check out the excellent permanent collection of Australian art. (p25)

NGV International Expansive permanent collection of international art including Rembrandt, Bacon and Picasso. (p48)

Hosier Lane Best known street-art laneway in the city. (p34)

Australian Centre for Contemporary Art Challenging contemporary art museum exhibiting local and international works. (p51)

Australian Centre for the Moving Image Well-curated collection of interactive exhibits relating to Australian TV and cinema. (p25)

Best Sights & Activities

Federation Square Learn about the city's prominent architectural square on a guided tour. (p24)

Birrarung Marr City park featuring indigenous flora, Aboriginal art and sculptures. (p26)

City Circle Tram Take a scenic ride through the city on a historic tram. (p35)

State Library of Victoria Admire the stunning La Trobe Reading Room and check out Ned Kelly's armour. (p34)

Shrine of Remembrance Take a guided tour of this war memorial with a returned soldier. (p72)

Best
Indigenous Culture

MICHAEL DODGE / GETTY IMAGES ©

While the Indigenous Wurundjeri people have inhabited Melbourne for around 50,000 years, sadly they make up a minute percentage of the population. Thankfully, however, in recent years there have been strong efforts to educate about and promote Wurundjeri culture and way of life through walking tours, artwork, or Indigenous-inspired cuisine. There are also museums detailing the devastation and hardships encountered with the arrival of European settlers.

Melbourne Museum Features the Bunjilaka Aboriginal Cultural Centre. (p110)

Ian Potter Centre: NGV Australia Extraordinarily beautiful collection of Aboriginal art. (p25)

Birrarung Marr City parkland incorporating Indigenous themes including art installations and stories of Wurundjeri people. (p26)

Charcoal Lane Restaurant showcasing Indigenous flavours from wallaby sirloin and emu fillet to wattleseed pavlova. (p99)

Koorie Heritage Trust A mix of an Indigenous museum, gallery and shop with tours of Flagstaff Gardens. (p37)

Aboriginal Heritage Walk Learn how the Wurundjeri lived on this walking tour through the Botanic Gardens. (p69)

State Library of Victoria Features exhibits that delve into first encounters of the Wurundjeri with colonial settlers and a controversial treaty signed with John Batman. (p34)

Bunjil A 23m-high sculpture inspired by Bunjil, the eagle-like Wurundjeri creator spirit. (p52)

Melbourne Cricket Ground Aussie Rules footy is an Indigenous game, and the surrounding MCG parkland is home to scar trees. (p82)

Best
Shopping

Melbourne's reputation as a shopping mecca is, we are pleased to announce, utterly justifiable. It's a city of passionate, dedicated retailers catering to a broad range of tastes, whims and lifestyles. From boutique-filled city laneways to suburban shopping streets and malls, you'll find plenty of places to offload your cash and pick up something unique.

Where to Shop

Smaller retailers and design workshops inhabit the city laneways, as well as the vertical villages of Curtin House and the Nicholas Building. Flinders Lane and the arcades and laneways that feed into it are particularly blessed. Chapel St has all the chain stores and classic Australian names at the South Yarra end, as well as some edgier designers once you hit Prahran. Look for streetwear in Greville St, Prahran, and in Windsor; the latter is also good for vintage shopping. Gertrude St, Fitzroy, mixes vintage with many of the city's most sought-after innovators, as well as up-and-coming menswear, art-supply shops and vintage furniture.

Melbourne Black

One constant in Melbourne fashion is colour, or lack of it. You'll not go long without hearing mention of 'Melbourne black', and it's true that inky shades are worn not just during the cold months but right through the hottest days of summer. Perhaps it's because black somehow suits the soft light and often grey days, or maybe it's the subliminal influence of the city's moody bluestone. In Melbourne, black is always the new black.

LONELY PLANET / GETTY IMAGES ©

Best Bookstores

Readings Local favourite indie bookstore with a great selection. (p121)

Books for Cooks Stocks an incredible range of gastronomic titles, local and global. (p103)

Polyester Books Perfect place to find zines, underground comics and music bios. (p105)

Best Food Stores

Gewürzhaus A chef's dream store with a great range of spices. (p31)

Prahran Market One of the best produce markets in the city. (p74)

Best Record Stores

Pure Pop Records Well-loved St Kilda local, also hosts gigs. (p133)

Esplanade Market

Greville Records A Prahran oldie with an excellent vinyl collection. (p79)

Best Markets

Rose Street Artists' Market Clever and crafty artists gather each weekend to sell their wares and talk shop. (p105)

Esplanade Market A range of handicrafts on sale with a seaside backdrop. (p125)

Queen Victoria Market From tacky souvenirs to delightful deli produce, this is the mummy and daddy of all Victorian markets. (p28)

Best Fashion

Alice Euphemia Quirky, art-school inspired pieces by local designers. (p45)

Gorman Geometric prints, organic tees and Scandinavian-style shoes. (p103)

ESS Japanese-designed conceptual pieces for individuality. (p104)

Best Local Designers

Craft Victoria Shop Excellent collection of locally handmade ceramics, textiles, jewellery and other beautiful goods. (p43)

Third Drawer Down Pick up a giant corn-cob stool or high-end art. (p103)

Rose Street Artists' Market Loads of stalls showing off the best in local design. (p105)

Best
Live
Entertainment

With a proud homegrown live-music scene and thriving classical, opera and dance, Melbourne is not short of entertainment options. Whether it's thrashing out to high-octane rock 'n' roll, nodding along to indie or taking in a performance of world-class classical music that you're looking for, the city has a full rotating calendar of events to suit everyone.

Dance

The **Australian Ballet** (☎1300 369 741; www.australian-ballet.com.au; 2 Kavanagh St, Southbank; 🚊1) is the national ballet company and considered one of the finest in the world. It performs regularly at Melbourne's Victorian Arts Centre, with a program of classical and modern ballets. Victoria's flagship contemporary dance company, Chunky Move, is a tidy package of bold, often confronting, choreography, pop-culture concepts, technically brilliant dancers, sleek design and smart marketing.

Opera

Ninety years after Nellie Melba was made a dame, classical music still has a strong presence in Melbourne. The Melbourne Symphony Orchestra performs works drawn from across the classical spectrum, from the popular to challenging contemporary composition. The orchestra is based at the recently renovated Arts Centre's Hamer Hall.

AMANDA HALL / GETTY IMAGES ©

☑ Top Tips

▶ Pick up a copy of free street magazines **Beat** (www.beat.com.au) or the **Music** (www.themusic.com.au) for upcoming gigs and news, or visit **Mess+Noise** (www.messandnoise.com) online forum for info on the local scene.

▶ **Half-Tix** (Melbourne Town Hall, cnr Little Collins & Swanston Sts) sells half-price tickets to shows and concerts on day of performance.

Best Live Music

Tote One of Melbourne's most legendary live-music venues, this Collingwood pub is all about raucous bands. (p102)

Australian Ballet

Esplanade Hotel A true St Kilda icon, the Espy is a temple to live music, with nightly acts. (p133)

Corner Hotel Richmond's classic band venue that's hosted a who's who of indie and rock bands. (p87)

Cherry Located on ACDC Lane, this city rock bar attracts a fun lovin' crowd of music fans. (p31)

Bennetts Lane The city's premier jazz venue attracts quality acts. (p42)

Night Cat Energetic, fun late-night venue with swinging funk, Latin and jazzy live bands. (p103)

Best Classical, Opera & Dance

Melbourne Symphony Orchestra World-class orchestra that mixes things up by accompanying acts from Kiss to Burt Bacharach. (p55)

Melbourne Opera Quality local performances in an attractive historical theatre with accessible prices. (p42)

Australian Ballet The nation's leading ballet company is based in Melbourne and performs at the Arts Centre. (p150)

Chunky Move Contemporary, cutting-edge dance company performing at Southbank's Australian Centre for Contemporary Art. (p54)

Kage Physical Theatre Mixing modern dance with theatre at the atmospheric Abbotsford Convent. (p107)

Worth a Trip

The stage at the **Northcote Social Club** (📞 03-9489 3917; www.northcote-socialclub.com; 301 High St, Northcote; 🕐 4pm-late Mon & Tue, noon-late Wed-Sun; 🚌 86, 🚉 Northcote), an inner-north favourite, has seen plenty of international folk just one album out from star status. The homegrown line-up is also notable. If you're just after a drink, the front bar buzzes every night of the week, and there's a large deck out back for lazy afternoons.

Best
Arcades & Laneways

Melbourne's atmospheric bluestone laneways mix European chic with New York grit and are home to hip bars, swanky restaurants and boutique shopping set up by local designers. It's also where Melbourne's world-renowned street-art scene has exploded with quality graffiti down hidden lanes. Its arcades meanwhile sparkle with 19th-century elegance and art nouveau features.

ANDREW WATSON / GETTY IMAGES ©

Best Street Art

Hosier Lane Melbourne's most renowned street-art location is an urban gallery of ever-changing murals, stencils and graffiti. (p34)

Rutledge Lane Leading off Hosier Lane, Rutledge has established itself as a site for emerging artists to practise their craft. (p31)

Blender Lane Close to the Queen Victoria Market, this unsigned laneway has edgy stencils and installments, and is home to Blender Studios. (p29)

Croft Alley An explosion of colour on this laneway's graffitied walls leads to a cool, hidden bar. (p30)

Best Drinking

Centre Place Pulling off mod and edgy, this quintessential bluestone Melbourne laneway has cool hidden bars, eateries and graffiti. (p31)

Degraves St Famous for its Parisian-style outdoor street-side cafes, great coffee and boutique stores. (p31)

Tattersalls Lane Passing through Chinatown, this laneway crams in hip bars (such as Section 8) in warehouses and shipping containers, and cheap tasty dumplings. (p42)

Best Entertainment

ACDC Lane It's a long way to the top of this laneway if you wanna rock 'n' roll; a must for music lovers, with Cherry bar at its end. (p31)

Carson Place Quirky Butterfly Club featuring offbeat theatre, comedy and a kitschy cocktail bar. (p31)

Best Historic Arcades

Block Arcade Oozing 19th-century European class, this sparkling complex features great shopping and stylish cafes. (p31)

Royal Arcade Charming and elegant, a boutique arcade that's a monument to 'marvellous' 19th-century Melbourne with its gleaming tiles and exquisite features. (p31)

Best
Gay & Lesbian

Melbourne's gay and lesbian community is well integrated into the general populace, but clubs and bars can be found in two distinct areas: Abbotsford and Collingwood in the inner north, and Prahran and South Yarra in the inner south. Commercial Rd, which separates Prahran and South Yarra, is home to a couple of gay clubs, cafes and businesses. It's more glamorous than the 'northside', which is regarded as more down to earth and less pretentious.

Festivals & Events

Plenty of Melbourne venues get into the spirit during Midsumma Festival (January to February). This diverse program of cultural, community and sporting events includes the popular Midsumma Carnival at Alexandra Gardens, St Kilda's Pride March and much more. Australia's largest GLBT film festival, the Melbourne Queer Film Festival, screens more than 100 films from around the world each March.

Best Venues

Kama Bar (☎03-9804 5771; www.facebook.com/ kamaclub; 119 Commercial Rd, South Yarra; ⊙5pm-late; 🚋72) The former Exchange Hotel, Kama Bar is one of the few remaining gay venues along Commerical Rd with regular DJs and drag shows.

Peel Hotel (☎03-9419 4762; www.thepeel.com. au; 113 Wellington St, Collingwood; ⊙9pm-dawn Thu-Sat; 🚋86) One of Melbourne's most famous gay venues, the Peel features a male crowd dancing to house music, retro and commercial dance. It's on Peel St, which runs east off Smith St.

Commercial Hotel (☎03-9689 9354; 238 Whitehall St, Yarraville; ⊙4pm-midnight Mon, to 11pm Tue, Wed & Sun, to 3am Thu-Sat) A friendly, low-key pub in Melbourne's inner west that presents drag shows on Saturday nights. From the CBD, follow Footscray Rd and turn left down Whitehall.

GH Hotel (Greyhound Hotel; ☎03-9534 4189; www.ghhotel.com.au; cnr Carlisle St & Brighton Rd, St Kilda; 🚋16, 67, 79) The old Greyhound's had a dramatic makeover; expect drag-filled evenings from Thursday to Saturday, and a nightclub with a state-of-the-art sound system.

Best
The Arts

Long regarded as the culture capital of Australia, Melbourne is a city for artists and art lovers. Its strong arts community and its passion for literature, theatre and visual arts provide a creative backdrop fundamental to the fabric of the city. The arts scene in Melbourne is highly accessible, both through the sheer number of art spaces and the appeal to a broad audience.

Visual Arts

Visual art is a prominent part of Melbourne's arts landscape. It thrives and grows in most places: tucked away in basement galleries, stencilled on unmarked laneway walls, proudly boasted from world-class museums and sneaking up on you in parks and gardens.

Contemporary Art

Between commercial, public and artist-run galleries, there is much to discover in Melbourne's contemporary arts scene. Tap into it at Gertrude Contemporary Art Space, which hosts exhibitions by emerging artists and fosters innovative and challenging ideas. The Australian Centre for Contemporary Art generates cutting-edge programs of exhibitions as well as developing large-scale projects with Australian and international artists.

Theatre

Melbourne's theatrical heritage is evident in the legacy of Victorian-era theatres such as the Princess and Athenaeum, and its most high-profile professional theatre company, the Melbourne Theatre Company (MTC), is also Australia's oldest. Humble in size, Carlton's La Mama (founded in 1967) is the mother of independent theatre in Melbourne.

KRZYSZTOF DYDYNSKI / GETTY IMAGES ©

☑ **Top Tip**

▶ Flinders Lane has the densest concentration of commercial galleries in Australia, and there are many more dotted throughout the city and inner suburbs. **Art Almanac** (www.art-almanac. com.au) has comprehensive listings.

NGV International

Best Theatre

Malthouse Theatre
Dedicated to promoting Australian works.
(p54)

Red Stitch Actors Theatre Tiny, independent St Kilda theatre. (p78)

La Mama Reputation for developing emerging playwrights. (p120)

Melbourne Theatre Company The city's major theatre company. (p55)

Best Contemporary Art

Australian Centre for Contemporary Art
Showcases local and international artists. (p51)

Centre for Contemporary Photography Not-for-profit with changing exhibitions. (p97)

Gertrude Contemporary Art Space Highly reputable not-for-profit. (p97)

Best Art Museums

Ian Potter Centre: NGV Australia Great collection of Australian and Indigenous art. (p25)

NGV International Hosts blockbuster shows by major names. (p48)

Worth a Trip

The former home of John and Sunday Reed, **Heide Museum of Modern Art** (☎ 03-9850 1500; www.heide.com. au; 7 Templestowe Rd, Bulleen; museum adult/child $16/free; ☉10am-5pm Tue-Sun; 🚌 903, 🚆 Heidelberg) is a public art gallery with wonderful grounds. Changing exhibitions include works by Sidney Nolan and Albert Tucker. Free tours (2pm) introduce Melbourne's early painting scene. Heide's signposted off the Eastern Fwy.

Best
Tours

Best Walking Tours

Melbourne by Foot
(☑0418 394 000; www.
melbournebyfoot.com; tours
$35; ☒Flinders St) Take a
few hours out and experi-
ence a mellow, informa-
tive walking tour that
covers street art, politics,
Melbourne's history and
diversity.

Hidden Secrets Tours
(☑03-9663 3358; www.
hiddensecretstours.com;
tours $95-195) Offers a
variety of walking tours
covering everything from
lanes and arcades to
wine, architecture, coffee
and cafes, and vintage
Melbourne.

St Kilda Music Walk-
ing Tours (SKMWT; www.
skmwt.com.au; tours
$40; ◷weekends) This
rock 'n' roll tour takes
in the infamous bars
and landmarks that
played starring roles in
St Kilda's underground
music scene. Led by St
Kilda music icons, including Fred Negro and Fiona
Lee Maynard.

Best Art Tours

Walk to Art (☑03-8415
0449; www.walktoart.com.
au; tours 2/4hr $78/108)
These walks take you
to galleries and artist-
run spaces hidden in
Melbourne's buildings
and laneways. Four-hour
tours run on Wednesday
and Saturday; there's a
two-hour express tour on
Friday.

Melbourne Street Art
Tours (☑03-9328 5556;
www.melbournestreettours.
com; tours $69; ◷1.30-
5pm Tue, Thu & Sat) Three
hour tours exploring the
street-art side of Mel-
bourne. The tour guides
are street artists them-
selves, so you'll get a
good insight into this art.

Scenic Tours

Global Ballooning
(☑1800 627 661; www.
globalballooning.com.au;
from $440) Wake up at
the crack of dawn to view
the city from another
angle on this one-hour
ride.

LINDSAY BROWN / GETTY IMAGES ©

Kayak Melbourne
(☑0418 106 427; www.
kayakmelbourne.com.au;
tours $72-118; ☒11, 31,
48) Don't miss out on
the chance to see Mel-
bourne's Yarra River by
kayak. Moonlight tours
are most evocative and
include a dinner of fish
and chips.

Survival Guide

Survival Guide

Before You Go

When to Go

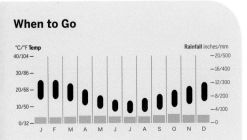

➤ Summer (Dec–Feb)
Balmy nights, Grand Slam tennis, cricket and plenty of events.

➤ Autumn (Mar–May)
Generally glorious weather as the Australian F1 Grand Prix rolls into town and the Moomba festival takes over the Yarra.

➤ Winter (Jun–Aug)
Escape the cold with gallery-hopping, and toasty live-music venues, and get rugged up at the footy with a thermos.

➤ Spring (Sep–Nov)
First signs of warm weather as footy finals fever hits before the hats are on and the horses are galloping during Spring Racing Carnival.

Book Your Stay

➤ Prices peak during the Australian Open in January, Grand Prix weekend in March, AFL footy finals in September and the Spring Racing Carnival in November.

➤ Midrange to deluxe hotels publish 'rack rates', but you should always ask for current specials.

➤ In addition to the usual chains, there are some excellent boutique choices, from art-themed hotels to 19th-century splendour and rock 'n' roll chic.

➤ Stylish, self-contained apartment-style rooms are increasingly common in the central business district (CBD) and inner city, and provide excellent value.

➤ There's an abundance of hostels in Melbourne, from generic backpackers to more character-filled places in historical buildings and well-equipped flashpackers.

Useful Websites

Lonely Planet (www.hotels.lonelyplanet.com) Author recommendations, reviews and online booking.

Visit Melbourne (www.visitmelbourne.com/accommodation) Accommodation listings and bookings for Melbourne and Victoria.

RACV (www.racv.com.au) Online booking for Melbourne and regional Victoria; publishes the *Accommodation Guide*.

Booking.com (www.booking.com) Online booking with good deals.

Best Budget

Space Hotel (www.spacehotel.com.au) Slick, modern and immaculate flashpacker option.

Nunnery (www.nunnery.com.au) Not your ordinary hostel, this Fitzroy stunner is within a former convent.

Habitat HQ (www.habitathq.com.au) Popular and social St Kilda hostel that's run like a tight ship.

Home@TheMansion (www.homemansion.com.au) Character-filled hostel in grand heritage building, close to city and Fitzroy.

Best Midrange

Alto Hotel on Bourke (www.altohotel.com.au) Smart, environmentally friendly city hotel.

Brooklyn Arts Hotel (www.brooklynartshotel.com.au) Quirky, historical hotel attracting artsy visitors looking for homely comfort.

Albany (www.thealbany.com.au) Midrange boutique hotel across from Fawkner Park on the edge of the city.

Prince (www.theprince.com.au) Chic St Kilda hotel with dramatic lobby and rooms featuring a pared-back aesthetic.

Best Top End

Ovolo (www.ovologroup.com) Boutique hotel mixes hipster chic with funky executive.

Art Series (Cullen) (www.artserieshotels.com.au/cullen) The coolest of the Art Series hotels, decked out with works by the late Adam Cullen.

Adelphi Hotel (www.adelphi.com.au) One of Australia's first boutique hotels has recently reopened with a five-star makeover.

Hotel Lindrum (www.hotellindrum.com.au) This attractive city hotel was once the snooker hall of the legendary Walter Lindrum.

Arriving in Melbourne

☑ **Top Tip** For the best way to get to your accommodation, see p17.

Melbourne Airport

Melbourne Airport (☎03-9297 1600; www.melbourneairport.com.au), often referred to as Tullamarine or Tulla, is around 25km northwest of the city centre. All international and domestic terminals are within the same complex. There are no direct train or tram services linking with the city, but airport shuttle buses meet flights and taxis descend like flies.

SkyBus (☎03-9335 2811; www.skybus.com.au; adult one-way $18) Has a 24-hour express service from Tullamarine Airport (20 to 30 minutes) to/from Southern Cross Station, departing every 10 to 30 minutes.

Taxis Cost from $50; around 20 minutes to the city.

Avalon Airport

Avalon Airport (☎03-5227 9100, 1800 282 566; www.avalonairport.com.au) lies around 55km southwest of the city centre on the way to Geelong. At the time of writing, only Jetstar flights to/from Sydney and Brisbane use the airport.

Sita Coaches (☎03-9689 7999; www.sitacoaches.com.au; adult/child $22/10) One way from Southern Cross Station to Avalon Airport takes 50 minutes.

Taxis Cost $80; around one hour to the city.

Southern Cross Station

Southern Cross Station (www.southerncrossstation.net.au; cnr Collins & Spencer Sts, Melbourne) is Melbourne's main terminal for long-distance trains and buses, and the arrival/departure point for airport buses. It's also a metro train station and has trams outside that connect it to the city centre, St Kilda and Fitzroy.

V/Line (☎1800 800 007; www.vline.com.au) Buses and trains around Victoria.

Firefly (☎1300 730 740; www.fireflyexpress.com.au) Buses to/from Adelaide and Sydney.

Greyhound (☎1300 473 946; www.greyhound.com.au) Buses Australia-wide.

Station Pier

The **Spirit of Tasmania** (☎1800 634 906; www.spiritoftasmania.com.au; adult/car one-way from $174/89) crosses Bass Strait from Melbourne to Devonport, Tasmania, at least nightly; there are also day sailings during peak season. It takes 11 hours and departs from Station Pier, Port Melbourne.

Getting Around

Tram

☑ **Best for...** Inner-city travel and cultural experiences.

Both iconic and useful, Melbourne's extensive network of tramlines covers every corner of the city, running north–south and east–west along most major roads. Trams run roughly every 10 minutes Monday to Friday, every 15 minutes on Saturday and every 20 minutes on Sunday.

➡ The free burgundy-coloured City Circle Tram (p35) loops around town and makes an excellent option for short jaunts within the city centre.

➡ Trams start from around 5am until midnight. Timetables are variable; expect a tram to rattle along every five to 20 minutes.

Train

☑ **Best for...** Getting around quickly and cheaply.

➡ Flinders Street Station is the main metro train station connecting the city and suburbs. The City Loop runs under the city, linking the four corners of town at Southern Cross, Flagstaff, Melbourne Central and Parliament. Melbourne's suburbs are also well connected.

➡ Trains begin around 5am and finish at midnight. Sunday services begin a little later.

➡ Trains run roughly every 10 to 30 minutes, depending on the time of day.

Bus

☑ **Best for...** Sightseeing on a visitor shuttle and travel in the suburbs.

➡ **Melbourne Visitor Shuttle** (Tourist Shuttle; www.thatsmelbourne.com. au; daily ticket $5, children under 10 free; ⏰ 9.30am-4.30pm) provides a good service for tourists with its 1½-hour round trip. The tour includes audio commentary and covers 13 stops that take passengers to all of Melbourne's main sights.

➡ Melbourne's regular buses are also handy for getting around town, especially if crossing suburbs, and can provide shortcuts on some inner-suburban routes such as from Collingwood to Brunswick.

Bicycle

☑ **Best for...** Short city jaunts, independence and saving money.

➡ **Melbourne Bike Share** (☎ 1300 711 590; www.mel-bournebikeshare.com.au) allows free bicycle rental for 30-minute trips, available from 51 bright-blue stations around the city. Bike helmets are compulsory under the law; subsidised safety helmets can be bought in the city centre from 7-Eleven stores ($5 with a $3 refund), though increasingly helmets are provided free with the bike. You can also rent bikes daily ($2.80) or weekly ($8).

➡ The **Humble Vintage** (☎ 0432 032 450; www. thehumblevintage.com) rents out vintage bikes for around $30 per day (with helmet and lock).

➡ Cycling maps are available from the Melbourne

Tickets & Passes

Melbourne's buses, trams and trains use myki, the controversial 'touch on, touch off' ticketing system. It's not particularly convenient for short-term visitors, and requires you to purchase a $6 plastic myki card and then put credit on it before you travel.

➡ Cards can be purchased from machines at stations, 7-Elevens or newsagents, but some hostels collect myki cards from travellers who leave Melbourne.

➡ The myki card can be topped up at 7-Eleven stores, machines at most train stations and at some CBD tram stops (frustratingly, online top-ups take at least 24 hours to process). Fines for not travelling with a valid myki are $212, and ticket inspectors are vigilant and unforgiving.

➡ Costs for zone 1 (which is all that most travellers will need): myki money two-hour $3.50, daily $7. Machines don't always issue change, so bring exact money.

➡ Contact **Public Transport Victoria** (PTV; ☎ 1800 800 007; www.ptv.vic.gov.au; Southern Cross Station; ☒ Southern Cross) for more information.

➡ Public transport runs from around 5am to 12.30am.

Visitor Centre at Federation Square and **Bicycle Victoria** (☎03-8376 8888; www.bv.com.au).

➡ Bikes can be taken on trains, but not on trams or buses.

Car & Motorcycle

☑ **Best for...** Independence and accessing outlying suburbs.

➡ Major car-hire companies are represented at the airport and central locations:

Avis (☎13 63 33; www.avis.com.au)

Budget (☎1300 362 848; www.budget.com.au)

Europcar (☎1300 131 390; www.europcar.com.au)

Hertz (☎13 30 39; www.hertz.com.au)

Rent a Bomb (☎13 15 53; www.rentabomb.com.au)

Thrifty (☎1300 367 227; www.thrifty.com.au)

➡ Both drivers and motorcyclists will need to purchase a toll pass if they're planning on using one of the two toll roads: **CityLink** (☎13 26 29; www.citylink.com.au), which runs from Tullamarine Airport to the city and eastern suburbs, or **EastLink**

(☎13 54 65; www.eastlink.com.au), which runs from Ringwood to Frankston. Pay online or via phone; pay within three days to avoid a fine.

➡ Driving is on the left-hand side of the road.

➡ Wearing seat belts is compulsory. Motorcyclists must wear crash helmets at all times.

➡ The police strictly enforce Victoria's blood-alcohol limit of 0.05% with random breath testing (and drug testing) of drivers.

➡ Foreign driving licences are valid as long as they are in English or accompanied by a translation. If in doubt, pick up an International Drivers Licence from your home country's automobile association.

➡ Car-sharing companies that operate in Melbourne include **Flexi Car** (☎1300 363 780; www.flexicar.com.au), **Go Get** (☎1300 769 389; www.goget.com.au) and **Green Share Car** (☎1300 575 878; www.greensharecar.com.au). You rent the cars by the hour (from $14) or the day (from $80) and prices include petrol. They vary on joining fees (free to $40) and how they

charge (insurance fees, per hour or per kilometre).

➡ Driving in the city is best avoided, but if you do be sure to abide by the 'hook turn' system, where right-turning motorists at signed intersections must turn from the left lane just as the lights turns red. This is to ensure trams aren't held up; keep an eye out for 'hook turn' signs at the top of tram lines.

Taxi

☑ **Best for...** Late nights, and when you have a group to share the costs.

Melbourne's yellow taxis are metered, and require an estimated prepaid fare when hailed between 10pm and 5am. You may need to pay more or get a refund depending on the final fare. Toll charges are added to fares.

➡ Taxi companies include **Silver Top** (☎131 008; www.silvertop.com.au) and **13 Cabs** (☎13 22 27; www.13cabs.com.au).

Water Taxis

☑ **Best for...** Scenic boat trips; getting to Williamstown and Docklands.

Slow going but an option, ferries service the Yarra and Maribyrnong

Rivers, from South-
gate to Richmond or
Williamstown.

➡ **Williamstown Ferries**
(☏03-9517 9444; www.
williamstownferries.com.au;
one-way Williamstown–Southbank adult/child $18/9)

➡ **Melbourne River
Cruises** (☏03-8610 2600;
www.melbcruises.com.au;
one-way Williamstown–city
centre adult/child $22/11)

➡ **Melbourne Water Taxis**
(☏0416 068 655; www.mel-
bournewatertaxis.com.au)

Essential Information

Business Hours

Banks 9.30am to 4pm
Monday to Thursday, to
5pm Friday

Post offices 9am to 5pm
Monday to Friday, 9am
to noon Saturdays some
branches

Tourist offices 9am to
5pm daily

Shopping centres 9am
to 5.30pm, often to 9pm
Thursdays and Fridays

Discount Cards

The **myki Visitor Pack**
($14; www.ptv.vic.gov.au/tick-
ets/myki/myki-visitor-pack)
is recommended for tour-
ists; it gets you one day's
travel and discounts on
various sights. Available
only from the airport,
SkyBus terminal or the
PTV Hub at Southern
Cross Station.

Electricity

220V/50Hz

Power supply is
240V/50Hz

Emergency

Police/fire/ambulance
(☏000)

Money

➡ Currency is the Australian dollar (AUD), which
is made up of 100 cents.
There are 5c, 10c, 20c,
50c, $1 and $2 coins, and
$5, $10, $20, $50 and
$100 notes.

➡ Most bank branches
have 24-hour ATMs and
will accept debit cards
linked to international
network systems, such as
Cirrus, Maestro, Visa and
MasterCard. Most banks
charge a fee (around $2
or 3%) for the privilege
of using their ATM if you
don't have an account
with them.

➡ Almost all retail outlets
have Eftpos, which allows
you to pay for purchases
electronically by card
without a fee.

➡ The most commonly
accepted credit cards
are Visa and MasterCard,
and to a lesser extent
American Express and
Diners Club. For lost or
stolen card services:

American Express
(☏1300 132 639)

Diners Club (☏1300 360
060)

MasterCard (☏1800
120 113)

Visa (☏1800 450 346)

Money-Saving Tips

➡ Melbourne Bike Share's free 30-minute usage (p161) is a good way of getting around the city.

➡ The free City Circle Tram (p35) loops around the city.

➡ Melbourne Visitor Shuttle (p161) tickets cost $5 and take you directly to all the sights.

➡ Self-contained apartments and hostels that have kitchens will save you costs on eating out. Markets have the best-value fresh produce.

➡ Change foreign currency at most larger banks or foreign exchange booths in the city and at Melbourne Airport's international terminal. Most large hotels will also change currency (or travellers cheques) for their guests, but the rate might not be as good as from other outlets.

➡ Tipping isn't obligatory in Australia, but it's certainly expected in city restaurants and cafes and is appreciated in Melbourne bars. Around 10% is standard at restaurants, with more for notable service.

Public Holidays

Victoria observes the following public holidays:

New Year's Day
1 January

Australia Day 26 January

Labour Day Second Monday in March

Good Friday, Easter Sunday, Easter Monday March/April

Anzac Day 25 April

Queen's Birthday Second Monday in June

Melbourne Cup Day First Tuesday in November (Melbourne only)

Christmas Day 25 December

Boxing Day 26 December

Safe Travel

➡ There are occasional reports of alcohol-fuelled violence in some parts of Melbourne's CBD, in particular King St, but generally Melbourne is a very safe city.

➡ Travelling on public transport without a valid ticket is taken very seriously by ticket inspectors.

Telephone

The increasingly elusive public payphone is either coin- or card-operated. Local calls are unlimited and cost 50c; calls to mobile phones are timed and attract higher charges. Some payphones accept credit cards; many don't work at all.

Mobile Phones

All Australian mobile phone numbers have four-digit prefixes beginning with ☎04. Australia's digital network is compatible with GSM 900 and 1800 handsets. Quadbased US phones will also work. Prepaid SIM cards are available from a range of telecommunications providers:

Dodo (www.dodo.com)

Optus (www.optus.com.au)

Telstra (www.telstra.com.au)

Virgin (www.virginmobile. com.au)

Vodafone (www.vodafone. com.au)

Phone Codes

Country code ☎61

Area code ☎03

International access code ☎0011

Directory assistance ☎1223

➡ Callers to Australia need to drop the first ☎0 in a mobile phone number and the ☎0 of the area code.

➡ Toll-free numbers begin with ☎1800. Phone numbers beginning with ☎13 or ☎1300 are the cost of a local call

Phonecards

There are a wide range of local and international phonecards available from most newsagents and post offices for a fixed dollar value (usually $5 to $50). These can be used with any public or private phone by dialling a toll-free access number and then the PIN on the card.

Toilets

Public toilets are found throughout Melbourne, including in major train stations and shopping centres. Most are free, though a few city-centre bathrooms charge.

Tourist Information

The **Melbourne Visitor Centre** (MVC; Map p32, E5; ☎03-9658 9658; www.melbourne.vic.gov.au/touristinformation; Federation Sq; ⏰9am-6pm; 🛜; 🚉Flinders St) at Federation Square has comprehensive tourist information on Melbourne and regional Victoria, including excellent resources for mobility impaired travellers, and a travel desk for accommodation and tour bookings. There are power sockets available, too, for recharging phones etc. There's also an information booth at Bourke St Mall (mostly for shopping and basic enquiries), and City Ambassadors, dressed in red, wander around the city and can help with info and directions.

Useful websites:

Visit Melbourne (www.visitmelbourne.com) Official tourist site.

That's Melbourne (www.thatsmelbourne.com.au) Downloadable maps, info and podcasts from the City of Melbourne.

Travellers with Disabilities

➡ Many of the attractions in Melbourne and regional Victoria are accessible for wheelchairs.

➡ Trains and newer trams have low steps to accommodate wheelchairs and people with limited mobility.

➡ Many car parks in the city have convenient spaces allocated for disabled drivers.

Dos & Don'ts

Do

➡ Drive on the left.

➡ Look right first when crossing the road.

➡ Always have a valid ticket for trains and trams.

Don't

➡ Get in the way of trams.

➡ Believe the weather forecast; it can go from hot to cold, dry to wet in no time.

➡ All pedestrian crossings feature sound cues and accessible buttons.

➡ **Travellers Aid** (Map p32, E4; ☎03-9654 2600; www.travellersaid.org.au; Level 3, 225 Bourke St) centres are particularly helpful to those with special needs and offer a variety of facilities to travellers.

➡ **City of Melbourne** (www. melbourne.vic.gov. au) has an online mobility map and information for people with disabilities.

Visas

All visitors to Australia need a visa – only New Zealand nationals are exempt, and even they receive a 'special category' visa on arrival. Application forms for the several types of visa are available from Australian diplomatic missions overseas, travel agents or the website of the **Department of Immigration & Citizenship** (www.immi.gov.au). If you are from a country not covered by either the eVisitor or ETA categories, or you want to stay longer than three months, you'll need to apply for a tourist visa. Working visas for those aged 18 to 30 are also available for many nationalities.

eVisitor

Many European passport holders are eligible for a free eVisitor visa, allowing stays in Australia for up to three months within a 12-month period. eVisitor visas must be applied for online (www.immi. gov.au/e_visa/evisitor. htm). They are electronically stored and linked to individual passport numbers, so no stamp in your passport is required. It's advisable to apply at least 14 days prior to your proposed date of travel to Australia.

Electronic Travel Authority (ETA)

Passport holders from eight countries that aren't part of the eVisitor scheme – Brunei, Canada, Hong Kong, Japan, Malaysia, Singapore, South Korea and the USA – can apply for either a visitor or business ETA. ETAs are valid for 12 months, with stays of up to three months on each visit. You can apply for the ETA online (www. eta.immi.gov.au), which attracts a nonrefundable service charge of $20.

Behind the Scenes

Send Us Your Feedback

We love to hear from travellers – your comments help make our books better. We read every word, and we guarantee that your feedback goes straight to the authors. Visit **lonelyplanet.com/contact** to submit your updates and suggestions.

Note: We may edit, reproduce and incorporate your comments in Lonely Planet products such as guidebooks, websites and digital products, so let us know if you don't want your comments reproduced or your name acknowledged. For a copy of our privacy policy visit lonelyplanet.com/privacy.

Trent & Kate's Thanks

Thanks to Maryanne Netto for giving us the chance to work on our hometown book. To commissioning editor Glenn van der Knijff, and cartographer Julie Sheridan, thanks for all of your hard work. Also, a shout out to destination editor Tasmin Waby for all of her work and assistance throughout the write-up of this project. We'd also like to thank our families, especially Gary and Heather, and Tim and Larysa for all of their help and support, plus a place to crash at times!

Acknowledgments

Photograph p26: Deborah Halpern's *Angel* (1988). Commissioned by the National Gallery of Victoria in collaboration with The Australian Bicentennial Authority and with the assistance of generous sponsors, 1988.

Cover photograph: Federation Square, Luigi Vaccarella/4Corners

This Book

This 3rd edition of Lonely Planet's *Pocket Melbourne* guidebook was researched and written by Trent Holden and Kate Morgan. The previous two editions were written by Donna Wheeler and Jayne D'Arcy. This guidebook was commissioned in Lonely Planet's Melbourne office, and produced by the following: **Commissioning Editors** Maryanne Netto, Glenn van der Knijff **Destination Editor** Tasmin Waby **Product Editor** Elin Berglund **Senior Cartographer** Julie Sheridan **Book Designer** Mazzy Prinsep **Assisting Editors** Susan Paterson, Gabrielle Stefanos **Assisting Cartographer** James Leversha **Cover Researcher** Naomi Parker **Thanks to** Anita Banh, Sasha Baskett, Ryan Evans, Larissa Frost, Corey Hutchison, Genesys India, Jouve India, Wayne Murphy, Karyn Noble, John Taufa, Tracy Whitmey, Juan Winata

Index

See also separate subindexes for:

⊗ **Eating p170**

⊕ **Drinking p171**

✪ **Entertainment p172**

⊕ **Shopping p172**

Our Writers

Trent Holden

Melbourne-born and -bred, Trent's a proud Victorian who's certain he lives in the best city in the world. A rabid AFL footy fan (carn the Hawks!) and cricket tragic, he's an equally passionate supporter of Melbourne's underground rock 'n' roll scene. He's also spent several years living down the Great Ocean Road and a stint in country Victoria in Trentham. This is Trent's 15th title for Lonely Planet, covering destinations across Asia and Africa.

Kate Morgan

Kate grew up in the southeastern suburb of Frankston before several years in the seaside suburb of St Kilda and finally crossing the river to the inner-north neighbourhood of Northcote. She's spent the past few years travelling the world writing guidebooks and has recently relocated to London as Lonely Planet's destination editor for western Europe. Kate loves coming home to Melbourne for a good coffee, the great live-music scene and trips down the Great Ocean Road.

Published by Lonely Planet Publications Pty Ltd
ABN 36 005 607 983
3rd edition – November 2014
ISBN 978 1 74220 214 3
© Lonely Planet 2014   Photographs © as indicated 2014
10 9 8 7 6 5 4 3 2 1
Printed in China